HOW TO FIND INFORMATION

A guide for researchers

SALLY RUMSEY

Open University Press

Open University Press
McGraw-Hill Education
McGraw-Hill House
Shoppenhangers Road
Maidenhead
Berkshire
England
SL6 2QL

email: enquiries@openup.co.uk
world wide web: www.openup.co.uk

and Two Penn Plaza, New York, NY 10121–2289, USA

First published 2004
Reprinted 2005

A catalogue record of this book is available from the British Library

ISBN 0 335 21428 2(pb) 0 335 21429 0(hb)

Library of Congress Cataloging-in-Publication Data
CIP data applied for

Typeset by YHT Ltd, London
Printed in the UK by Bell & Bain Ltd, Glasgow

CONTENTS

LIST OF FIGURES

LIST OF TABLES

LIST OF ABBREVIATIONS

AHRB	Arts and Humanities Research Board
APA	American Psychological Association
BNB	British National Bibliography
BOPCRIS	British Official Publications Collaborative Reader Information Service
BUBL	Bulletin Board for Libraries (full name no longer used)
CD	Compact Disc
CD-ROM	Compact Disc – Read Only Memory
COPAC	CURL OPAC
CORDIS	Community Research and Development Information Service
COS	Community of Science
CSA	Cambridge Scientific Abstracts
CURL	Consortium of University Research Libraries
DAI	Dissertation Abstracts International
DDC	Dewey Decimal Classification
DOAJ	Directory of Open Access Journals
DOI	Digital Object Identifiers
DVD	Digital Versatile Disc
ETD	Electronic Theses and Dissertations
EU	European Union
HE	Higher Education

HERO	Higher Education Research Opportunities
ICT	Information and Communication Technology
IE	Information Environment (JISC)
IEEE	Institute of Electrical and Electronics Engineers
ILL	Interlibrary Loan
IP	Intellectual Property, or Internet Protocol
ISBN	International Standard Book Number
ISO	International Organization for Standardization
ISSN	International Standard Serial Number
JISC	Joint Information Systems Committee
LC	Library of Congress
LCSH	Library of Congress Subject Headings
MeSH	Medical Subject Headings
NERC	Natural Environment Research Council
OAI	Open Archives Initiative
OPAC	Online Public Access Catalogue
PC	Personal Computer
PDF	Portable Document Format
PhD	Doctor of Philosophy
PLoS	Public Library of Science
PRO	Public Record Office
RAE	Research Assessment Exercise
RCUK	Research Councils UK
RDN	Resource Discovery Network
RSLG	Research Support Libraries Group
RSLP	Research Support Libraries Programme
SIGLE	System for Information on Grey Literature in Europe
SOSIG	Social Sciences Information Gateway
URL	Uniform Resource Locator
WoK	Web of Knowledge
WWW	World Wide Web

FOREWORD

At the heart of the research enterprise lies an absolute requirement to discover what other material has been published on the topic under study. Despite this fact few practical manuals exist to help the newcomer, or the more experienced researcher, find their way through all the complexities and hurdles that exist. That is what makes the present book so valuable, and I predict it will become an important adjunct on every researcher's desk. Rather like learning statistics, what a researcher needs is a volume with practical advice that can be turned to on a regular basis.

The book is also timely since the provision of 'research information resources' through local research libraries in individual universities or research institutes is undergoing great change, largely as a result of the electronic revolution. Much material can now be accessed directly at the desk top and – for the researcher – is proving a considerable boon. But there are dangers that published material will be missed and so access to search engines and databases is vital. It is here in particular that difficulties exist since few seamless means of identifying all the various sources exist. If one is fortunate then a single Web site will suffice, but that is rare in any branch of research.

As one reads this book it becomes ever more apparent that strenuous efforts are needed to stitch together the various strands, and that lies behind the recommendations to create a UK

Research Libraries Network (RLN) which arose from the report of the Research Support Libraries Group. The RLN starts work, based at the British Library, in April 2004.

The aims of this network, of all the librarians across the world, and most importantly of this manual are to make the ever-growing complexity easier to understand and to navigate.

Brian K. Follett
Chair of the UK Research Libraries Support Group

PREFACE

This book is primarily aimed at those undertaking academic research at post-doctoral, doctoral and masters level, but will also be useful to those working on final-year undergraduate projects. Those in research institutions or public sector bodies, information seekers in commercial settings (for example, a law firm) and professionals wishing to keep up to date in their subjects will also find it helpful, as will anyone faced with writing a report, advising members of an organization or using a commercial information centre.

What is information? In the context of this book, it is any resource such as a document, book, or other format required by the researcher that informs, and contributes to extending their knowledge. It may be bibliographic information necessary for tracking down documents. It may be data, an historical book or a paper not yet given at a conference written by a subject specialist. It could be a list of online subject gateways compiled by someone with knowledge of the subject area. It might be in electronic or a tangible format. It could be about a specialized subject area or a common, everyday topic.

And what about information overload? This term is of cold comfort to someone working in a subject where little has been written or who cannot find or access the information they need for their research. It is the *relevance* of information that is crucial –

the right information available from the most appropriate source at the right time.

Finding information is one thing: working out what information is required in the first place, knowing where to look for it, how to recognize it when it is discovered, how to get hold of it and then what to do with it are equally necessary. This book works through the skills and tools required by the researcher to achieve these ends. It deals mainly with electronic services and resources, although other formats are included.

The content is built on the following framework:

- deciding what information is required
- finding details of what is available
- obtaining the required information
- managing and using that information

The building blocks for information seeking are explained and a controlled, logical approach to information gathering is expounded. Serendipity plays an important role in the discovery of interesting and relevant sources which begs the question, is information retrieval an art or a science? One can be logical and methodical to a point, but, because every situation is different, one cannot be completely prescriptive about the methods. The researcher's experience built up over a period of time coupled with some lateral thinking (and a pinch of luck) all add to the process.

Some online resources offer two types of search facility: simple and advanced. Advanced searching implies the construction of long, complex search queries incorporating numerous devices such as truncation and proximity symbols. Perhaps so. Alternatively, advanced searching can be defined as knowing how to articulate a problem, then search for, locate and access relevant information using a broad spectrum of appropriate resources.

Although designed to be reasonably comprehensive, some topics are inevitably dealt with in more detail than others. However, I have attempted to include enough detail to give readers a good start in all topics. With so much overlap in some areas it has been difficult at times to divide the content into discrete headings. In addition, the book is generic, that is, not focused on one particular discipline. It is the underlying techniques that are the mainstay of the text, and so examples are drawn from many subjects. It is not a guidebook to using the Internet, nor is it about the technical details of electronic resources.

Inevitably a book concerned with electronic resources directs the reader to Web sites. The ephemeral nature of the Web is well known, but I have chosen to include selected sites despite the danger that some may disappear or change within the lifetime of the book. Web addresses are listed separately and indicated using superscript numbering.

This book grew out of efforts to improve library provision for researchers at the University of Surrey, and its federal partner, the University of Surrey Roehampton. It is also the result of experience of working with academic staff and students in attempting to ease the sometimes painful task of finding the information required for research in diverse and often highly specialized fields.

There are vast differences in the confidence and expertise of researchers in their ability to find what they need. Some are extremely competent with a well-developed knowledge of use of connectors and creating search queries. Others have muddled along, never having been formally enlightened as to how or where to look. Christopher West in his response to a report by the Research Support Libraries Group (RSLG 2003) noted that 'the implication is that all HE researchers arrive, like Botticelli's *Venus*, fully-formed with advanced information skills and that they are then completely purposive and efficient in the investigation of their information environments. Everyone who works in HE libraries knows that this isn't the case, even for academic staff' (West 2002: 146). This book goes some way towards rectifying this situation.

Sally Rumsey
Guildford, March 2004

ACKNOWLEDGEMENTS

I am grateful to the following for allowing me to quote extracts from their publications:

- BioMed Central for use of an extract from the BioMed Central Web site in Chapter 17
- The Buzan Organisation Ltd for permission to use its registered trade mark Mind Map®
- CAUL (Council of Australian University Librarians) for use of extracts from the ADT (Australian Digital Theses) programme Web site in Chapter 11
- Cambridge Scientific Abstracts for use of the record from *Sociological Abstracts* in Chapter 6
- The Higher Education Funding Council of England (HEFCE) for use of the RSLG (Research Support Libraries Group) report in the Preface and Chapters 6, 9 and 17
- Members of the ZBLSA project team for permission to use the concept of the diagram illustrating the link between resource discovery and resource access in Chapter 9
- The RED (Roehampton Educational Development) Centre for allowing me to use their advice on plagiarism in Chapter 15
- Richard Waller (editor) and authors at *Ariadne* (UKOLN online journal) for permission to use extracts from articles published in *Ariadne*

The book grew out of work on the *Researcher's Gateway*, a dedicated Web site at the University of Surrey, and the *Researcher's Companion*, an online tutorial in information retrieval for researchers. Development of this tutorial would not have been possible without the expert input from Academic Liaison Librarians and Academic Liaison Officers at the University Library, University of Surrey and the Information Resource Centre at the University of Surrey Roehampton. I should particularly like to thank Julie Mills, my counterpart at Roehampton, and Nadine Bannister for being such a model research assistant and making collaborative work so straightforward, even when separated by 25 miles of the A3.

Jennifer Nordon, Academic Services Manager and Deputy Head of Library Services at the University of Surrey, has been a constant support over the last four years, especially during the writing of this text.

Tom Korolewicz gave his valuable time to read and comment on the manuscript, for which I am extremely grateful.

Pauline and Steve Johnson provided valuable help by testing the index at very short notice.

None of this would have been possible without Robert Hall, Head of Library Services at the University of Surrey, who offered encouragement and advice from the start, as well as reading and commenting on the manuscript.

I should especially like to thank Liz Lyon, Director of UKOLN, who not only provided expert advice on current developments in scholarly communication, but gave me my first opportunities to work on library research projects.

I have been fortunate that willing specialists have read and commented on the manuscript. If any errors remain, they are my responsibility.

● 1

THE INFORMATION-GATHERING PROCESS

The process

The most successful information-gathering operations require a great deal of thought and the ability to work through each stage meticulously.

The process of information gathering comprises a series of steps. However, this process is an art rather than a science: the researcher may not follow all the steps for every enquiry; guidelines can be given, but circumstances may dictate changes in direction; the researcher will return to previous steps during the course of their investigations; serendipity will play a part.

The process of finding, accessing and handling information can be summarized as follows:

- Analysing the question or problem
- Defining the scope of the research and what information is required
- Identifying sources of that information (resource discovery)
- Finding where that information is stored (resource location)
- Gaining access to that information
- Ensuring that the information retrieved is a) what is required b) reliable (and possibly c) current)
- Managing searches and results
- Keeping up to date and monitoring new developments

which can be further broken down into:

- analysing
- defining
- identifying/discovering
- locating
- accessing
- evaluating
- managing
- updating

Although summarized numerically, the process is more circular than linear for large projects because of the heuristic nature of the work and the need to supplement what has been found with new discoveries. See Figure 1.1.

The skills required by the researcher

The research process can be carried out efficiently and effectively providing the researcher has the necessary skills. The principal skills required by the researcher are:

- analytical
- planning

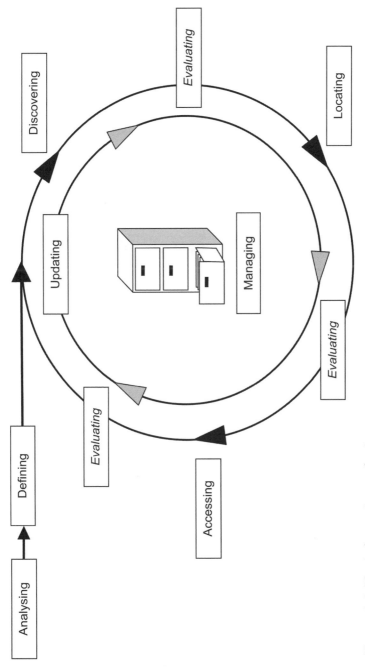

Figure 1.1 The information-gathering process

- searching (to know how and where to search)
- evaluation
- organizational

This book is designed to encourage the development of expert information-researching skills.

Defining the subject

It may seem obvious, but before starting research, it is vital that the researcher is clear about what it is they are setting out to achieve. The original title (or problem) may have been decided by a third party, or the researcher may have set their own topic. Either way, the researcher should check that the title is meaningful and unambiguous: if not, clarification is required (for those undertaking doctoral research, a supervisor may offer guidance). It can be helpful to write down the title and work through the following, making changes as appropriate:

- Examine the words used. Do they describe exactly what is being researched?
- Is there any ambiguity at all?
- Phrase the title/topic/main subject as a question (making sure the question retains relevance and covers all the areas intended). This can help the researcher define what it is they are actually doing.

Examples of titles and questions might be:

1. Changes in the Russian manufacturing industry since the formation of the new Federation.
   - What is the history and current state of the Russian manufacturing industry?
   - How has the Russian manufacturing industry changed since the formation of the new Federation?
2. 'The evolution of hominid dietary adaptations linked with environmental changes: extending the record beyond 100,000 years' (Richards 2002).

- Making reference to environmental changes, how has the hominid diet adapted and evolved beyond 100,000 years?
- How have environmental changes affected the evolution of hominid dietary adaptations beyond 100,000 years?
3. 'A pharmacy service for prisoners' (Department of Health 2003)
   - What is the current situation regarding pharmacy services for prisoners and how might they be improved?
4. 'Studies on the genomes of wild-type and vaccine strains of yellow fever virus' (Wang 1995)
   - What can we discover about the genomes of wild-type and vaccine strains of yellow fever virus?

The emphasis of the research will dictate the exact questions. The re-wording of the original title into a question leads to further questions such as:

- What information will I need to be able to answer this question?
- Where will I find that information?
- How can I find out about other research in this subject area?

and so on. How to answer these and other questions will be dealt with in later chapters.

Defining the purpose and scope of the research

Answers to the following will have a bearing on how to handle the finding and accessing process. Spending some time considering these issues will help define the nature and extent of the research, which will then dictate how to plan and execute the information retrieval.

- What or who is the information for?
- What type of document will the finished product be? (for example, doctoral **thesis**, company report)
- What level of detail is necessary?
- Who will use or read the finished product?

- How much information is to be retrieved? Everything ever published on the topic? Key texts? A single **item**?
- How much time is available? Is this a large-scale, long-term project, a short essay or something more immediate?
- How current does the information need to be? Legal information may need to be that which was made available this morning; an overview of a subject may be considering historical changes over a period of time. Beware of outdated or discredited materials.
- How far would I be prepared to travel to access resources? (specialist archives; records offices; museums; research libraries)
- How much am I willing to spend? (for example, the cost of document supply above any company or library allowance; travel; duplication and printing)
- What am I entitled to use? (for example, there may be access restrictions and other barriers such as those resulting from the Freedom of Information or Data Protection Acts)
- Where do I start?

Setting up and getting started

The successful researcher will do their preparation before embarking on the main task. This will include investigations at the home library/ies:

- finding out loan and other entitlements
- obtaining a current library card or equivalent
- obtaining any necessary usernames and passwords
- identifying an appropriate librarian or other individual who may be able to offer help
- identifying available services (such as interlibrary loan or other document supply or reciprocal borrowing arrangements at other libraries)
- checking opening hours and other practicalities
- finding out about the equipment (both hardware and software) needed to carry out the information-seeking and management process:

- checking Internet access
- obtaining word-processing and/or other software
- accessing bibliographic software or other reference management system
- printing facilities

The list of needs will depend on each individual case and should be compiled at the outset. Undoubtedly, needs will change during the course of the work, but having the basics available and functioning from the start can save problems later on.

Plan of campaign

The planning for information gathering can be likened to a military operation. A general might gather intelligence reports from informers, identify the strategic targets, plan the provision of food and transport and other facilities for the army, prepare a battle plan, review the situation hourly and act accordingly, and keep the commanders informed of the current and future situations. Similar tasks can be undertaken by a researcher for a successful and comprehensive outcome: meticulous planning, review and updating. This military-style planning can be vital; stumbling across appropriate information is possible and can retrieve welcome sources, but not reliable. Figure 1.2 shows the information-gathering process and how the different stages interrelate.

As stated above, the process will vary depending on the nature and extent of the research. For example, a person requiring a brief overview of a topic will probably want to identify and obtain a small number of key sources in a short time period. They may omit certain stages of the full process.

An important aspect of the information searching and retrieval process that needs stressing is its iterative (that is, repeating the process) and heuristic (that is, finding out as the process progresses and learning from what is discovered) nature. The more the researcher discovers, the more it leads to other sources. The key is not to become side-tracked into areas outside the remit, but remain on-task and follow up only relevant leads. As time

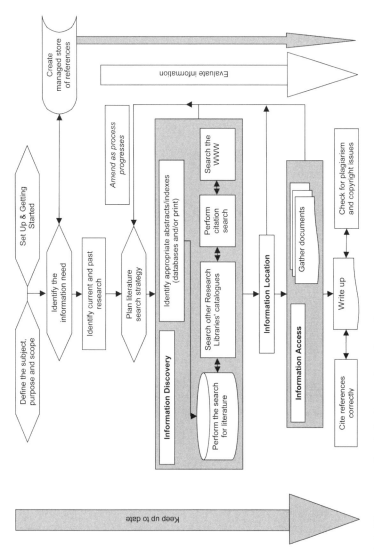

Figure 1.2 The researcher's information flowchart

progresses and the situation changes, so the researcher should be able to adapt to and monitor the changing landscape.

Having defined the subject and information needs and made the necessary preparations for information gathering, the researcher is ready to begin.

Key points

- Ensure clarity in what the research is about
- Be clear about who the final product is aimed at and the extent of the research
- Make sure all practical considerations are dealt with

2

USING A LIBRARY

Chapter outline

- Getting to know your library and librarian
- Library resources
- Library services
- The organization of resources in a library
- Using a library catalogue

Getting to know your library and librarian

Introduction

Libraries range from those confined to an intimate room with a single member of staff to large, split-site collections being used by thousands of people. Whatever the type, the researcher needs to be able to find what is required efficiently. This demands an ability to use the facilities for scrutinizing the holdings and to locate the items required. It is necessary to know the services on offer and where to go or who to turn to for help.

A library by any other name

Since the mid-1980s there has been a move away from the traditional term 'library' in an attempt to reflect the other services and resources that these centres now offer. Some provide combined Library and ICT (information and communication technology) services. Many libraries have abandoned the word and adopted terms such as:

- Learning Resource Centre
- Information Service
- Learning Centre

> In this book, the term 'library' is used to imply any department or centre that provides access to information for the purpose of research.

Orientation

Library staff may provide a personal tour of the building(s). An alternative may be a virtual tour, for example using a video presentation. Whatever the method, it is advisable to become familiar with the building and collections of any library of which one is expecting to make repeated use.

Some libraries operate on multiple sites and users should find out about the method of movement of stock between the sites, the **collections** and the services offered by each site. There may be differences in opening times and in the specialisms of the staff as well as the collections.

Libraries vary in their provision of ICT resources and workstations. It may be necessary to log-on using a network username and password: some may have computers with Internet access that are available to anyone. Some will provide laptop zones or wireless networking for use with personal portable computers. These are all issues that a visitor to a library may need to consider in order to make best use of the resources on offer.

Some university libraries provide a quiet section of the library with networked computers for the sole use of researchers. This has the advantage of being separated from the noise and bustle of the open access computers.

The emphasis of the collection

Although many libraries contain eclectic collections covering all or most subject areas in a variety of depths, many focus their collections on particular areas, defined by their users' interests. There are those that build up archive collections and those that focus solely on current interests.

Specialist collections

There are a large number of specialist libraries that have either extensive collections in one or more subject areas. For example, the British Library of Political and Economic Science is the 'world's largest social sciences library' (LSE 2004) and the Wellcome Library for the History and Understanding of Medicine 'preserves the record of medicine past and present' (Wellcome Library 2004). Some retain small collections of rare materials which may not be **open access**, but researchers might be able to obtain access either via their own library or by making an appointment directly with the specialist library.

It is vital that researchers are aware of specialist collections in their subject field. A useful publication is the *Aslib Directory of Information Sources in the United Kingdom* (Reynard 2002), which gives details of information sources by subject area, has a comprehensive index and includes contact details. Many large libraries stock this publication as well as others listing information sources in specific subject areas.

The M25 Consortium[1] categorizes collections at participating libraries by subject and HERO (Higher Education and Research Opportunities)[2] provides links to libraries both in the UK and abroad (including many of those mentioned below). A useful developing site is that of the London Libraries Development Agency[3].

Legal deposit

There are six libraries that are entitled to a copy of every item published in the UK:

* The British Library[4]
* Bodleian Library, Oxford
* National Library of Scotland, Edinburgh
* National Library of Wales, Aberystwyth
* Trinity College, Dublin
* University Library, Cambridge

Because of their extensive collections, these libraries can be of immense value to researchers, although there are restrictions on access (see also Chapters 9 and 11).

Unlike the other five who claim copies of items, publishers are obliged to send a copy of their publications to the British Library. Even though it is geographically in the Republic of Ireland, an historical agreement entitles Trinity College, Dublin to the legal deposit of items published in the UK. There is no national library in Northern Ireland, a situation that is likely to continue for the foreseeable future, as the UK government dismissed the idea of creating a new legal deposit library in the province following a 1997 consultation paper.

The Legal Deposit Libraries Act 2003 updated previous legislation so that electronic publications will in future be included in the legal deposit process. This will add greatly to the scholarly literature and preserve a vast additional corpus of information.

The hybrid library

The library is predominantly a point of access to information, whether the information is in print, an audio recording, in digital format, or any other storage medium and stored, say, on a remote Web server or obtained from another external source. Libraries' responsibilities extend to:

* negotiating licensing agreements and subscriptions with database suppliers

- arranging **document delivery** services with external bodies
- managing and arranging collaborative access and borrowing schemes with other institutions
- providing training (face to face and online) for users in using library resources
- providing study space
- provision of finding aids

and so on.

The library's presence on the Web

Most major libraries have large and comprehensive Web sites. These sites usually include details of resources and services and a link to the library's catalogue. However, not all smaller libraries have their own Web site. This means that the researcher who may be used to finding much of what they require on the WWW (World Wide Web), has to resort to use of the telephone, post, e-mail or a personal visit to find out more about the library and its collection(s).

A number of university libraries offer a section of their Web pages dedicated to doctoral and post-doctoral researchers, for example the *Researcher's Gateway*[5] at the University of Surrey.

Who to contact

For general enquiries there is usually some form of information desk or helpdesk. Alternatively, many queries can be answered using the library's Web site or information leaflets.

Any researcher who uses one or more libraries frequently would be well advised to get to know an appropriate member of staff. This might be a librarian with knowledge of resources available in a particular subject area. Some libraries appoint a member of staff as research support librarian whose job it is to concentrate solely on library provision for researchers.

The researcher may be able to spend some time with the librarian, discussing their personal information requirements and obtaining advice regarding the availability and use of library resources. The librarian will be aware of other sources of information, outside the home library, in their subject area(s).

The titles of librarians vary between institutions. Researchers may come across the following: subject librarian; information professional; learning advisor; liaison librarian; information officer; resources officer; or other variation.

In this book, the term 'librarian' is used for any information professional who advises researchers.

Helpdesk/information desk

All libraries have some form of help service for their users. This may take the form of a permanently staffed information desk, a *Frequently Asked Questions* kiosk or library enquiry e-mail service. If the library is run by a single person, it is unlikely that the librarian will be available to answer queries at all times. In a large library, an in-depth reference query will often be referred to the appropriate specialist member of staff.

Training

Librarians are usually keen to help users find the information they require. Often this is by enabling them to find what they need for themselves. Being able to discover, access and manage information efficiently and effectively is commonly called information literacy and the task of training users in these skills is usually the responsibility of librarians.

Because information is provided by an endless list of providers in a variety of formats via different interfaces, all researchers will benefit from advice from an information professional who specializes in information seeking and retrieval. It is recommended that researchers take advantage of any training available to them. Once learned, these skills can be adapted to different settings and can save much time and frustration. Training in library and information skills may be included as part of a doctoral or other academic programme or offered to employees.

Free access versus authenticated access

The WWW enables convenient and flexible access to **electronic resources**. Libraries frequently have an impressive array of electronic resources to which they provide access. These may be databases, e-journals, datasets or other materials. The benefits of electronic provision of these items include flexible and expert search options and access by multiple **concurrent users** on and off site at any time. Access may be via **subscription**, be conditional or **freely available**.

However, just because a document is accessible via the Internet does not imply that anyone is eligible to access it. Increasingly, reliable information is becoming freely available and there are many free information sources that are excellent in both content and organization (although there are others which are somewhat dubious). For example, the UK Government has made many of the publications and figures published by the Office for National Statistics (ONS 2004) freely available on the WWW. However, for many commercial resources, the institution will pay a subscription on behalf of the user who has to prove their eligibility to access the information, usually by use of a username and password. **Licensing** terms are strict, and sanctions against institutions that contravene the agreement can be punitive, so libraries manage access arrangements carefully. These licensing agreements contain restrictions such as:

- the user may not be able to use the database for any commercial use if the agreement is for educational use only (this can include students who go on industrial placements and still have access to their university/college electronic resources)
- not allowing publication of passwords to a third party
- the licence covers members of the named institution, so even if a researcher pays to join another library as an external member, it is unlikely they will be able to access the electronic resources

- use by a set number of concurrent users. When this limit is exceeded, other users cannot access the resource
- depending on the format and/or the licensing agreement, access may be limited to on-site users

For information sources that require payment, libraries and information centres will select those that are relevant to their users and which they can afford.

A word about passwords

Passwords can be a source of frustration and confusion to users. Their use abounds, not only in the research-seeking world, but in life in general. One of the main problems is that of having to cope with many different passwords. The **Athens** system used in UK higher and further education and other bodies attempts to address this problem by providing a single username and password as a means of access to multiple compliant resources.

The Athens system is becoming more streamlined as Single Sign On (SSO) gains popularity with information providers. This means the user can sign on to a resource using their Athens username and password, but does not have to repeat this process when transferring to another Athens compliant resource in the same session. The JISC (Joint Information Systems Committee) is committed to funding the Athens access management scheme until 2006. Work has begun to develop the next generation of access control methods such as the Shibboleth and Permis systems.

Not all resources are authenticated by Athens, so users often have to cope with other specially set passwords. These passwords can be difficult to manage as they have to be available for consultation by eligible users, but remain secret to everyone else. This can result in having to provide a password to find out what the correct password is for a resource! These passwords need changing regularly so that the resource remains accessible only to those who have the right of access.

Library resources

A collection may comprise items in one, some, or all of the following categories:

- Hard copy (including print resources including books, journals, maps, manuscripts)
- Electronic (including databases, CD-ROMs, DVD and other formats)
- **Microform** (microfilm, microfiche and microprint)
- Multimedia (including video, audio cassette, vinyl disc, film, photographs)
- Artefacts (including teaching resources, geological specimens, toys)

The researcher may or may not know the type of resource they require, but they will need to become familiar in how to use the formats in which the information they need is stored. Sometimes there is a choice of format and the most appropriate should be selected. For example, if there were a choice between a CD-ROM or Internet-based version, the Internet version might be more current. Likewise, the hard copy of a newspaper may be preferable if the online version does not include all the diagrams that accompany the article.

Library services

The issue desk

The issue desk is often the main front-line service of the library. This is where users borrow and return items and carry out other transactions such as placing reservations or collecting reserved items. Many libraries provide a self-service issue and returns facility to supplement the staffed issue desk.

Researchers should be aware of their **loan entitlement** (such as numbers of items and length of loan) and any restrictions that apply so that they can make full use of the library and its resources. Being aware of borrowing rights and observing due dates can save time and expense by avoiding withdrawal of privileges and unnecessary fines.

Interlibrary loans (ILL) and document supply

If access to an item is not provided either physically or electronically by the home library, a solution can be a document delivery service. For many libraries this is made possible using their **interlibrary loan** service. The researcher should be familiar with the procedures for ILL and document supply at their home library. This should include their allowance (these services are charged to libraries and so there is usually a set quota per person or fee per item) and the ability to obtain extra items for payment. Time allowances should be made for obtaining items not held by the home library (see Chapter 11).

Services for those with special needs

Libraries can be inhospitable places for those with physical or learning difficulties. Users may encounter difficulties with the buildings or with access to and use of the resources. Libraries are developing ways in which they can solve, or at least ease, such problems.

Intermediaries who liaise with the library

Depending on the institution, there may be a body such as a student advice service that assesses the needs of the individual and negotiates additional services or use of specialist technology for that person.

Specialist technology and adaptation of Web sites

Increasingly sophisticated technology is being developed for use by those who have special needs and libraries are increasing their provision of such equipment. The technology may include:

- specialist hardware such as Braille machines, large visual display units, adapted keyboards
- provision of standard hardware that eases the situation for those with difficulties – for example, scanners or colour printers
- specialist software such as a Mind Mapping program® or screen readers
- adaptation of Web pages, for example a text-only version and facilities such as user selection of background colours

Additional library services

Some libraries run additional services for those who require them. These may include such services as a fetch and collect service to save the user from having to navigate through a large building, negotiate shelving stacks and/or use a complex **classification system**.

The organization of resources in a library

The resources stored in a library may be sorted by subject or by some other criteria. Whatever the method, the library's **catalogue** is the key to finding what is available (including electronic resources) and the **shelfmark** (or **call number**) which is assigned to each physical item to locate it, either by the user, or by requesting the item via a member of library staff. The aim of such schemes is to aid efficient retrieval of items.

Open or closed access

Libraries vary in the amount of access they allow their users. Some are open access and have all their stock on display for users to handle and browse. These libraries are inclined to use a classification system that groups stock according to subject content. **Closed access** libraries require that users request items and wait whilst a member of staff fetches them. Many are a combination of the two. If a user requires closed access items they should leave ample time for ordering and collection. Depending on the location of the closed access items, there may only be a few collections per day during office hours.

Browse or search

A closed access collection demands that the user search the catalogue for relevant items. Open access gives some choice. If the choice is available, the user should scour the catalogue for all the relevant items they can discover. Having found the appropriate shelfmarks, it can be beneficial to peruse the shelves in those areas as there is always the possibility that relevant titles on a similar topic have been overlooked when searching. This is particularly true of items that use unexpected words in their titles or records, or for catalogues that have a limited subject searching facility.

The classification system

In a library, classification is the means of grouping items by subject area. It is the task of the classifier to assign a classification number to each item so that it can be shelved in an orderly fashion according to subject and, just as importantly, easily retrieved by users.

Serials may be shelved separately, perhaps without using a classification system. For example, they may be shelved in alphabetical order of title.

The subject nature of classification

Use of a classification system such as Dewey decimal classification (see below) should, in theory, result in items in a similar subject area being shelved in close proximity.

However, in practice browsing should not be relied upon. As classification is more an art than a science, the location of an item is dependent on the classifier. For example, a book on the psychological impact of medical treatment could either be shelved with others on psychology or with those on medicine. Also, when a classification system is updated, as they are from time to time, the result may be that items are shelved at more than one number and the library has to consider whether or not to renumber large amounts of stock. To counter these problems the library's catalogue should always be used to check the correct locations.

Methods of classification

There are a number of systems in use in libraries and users may need to become familiar with one or more of them. They vary from the well-known Dewey Decimal Classification (DDC) and Library of Congress (LC) systems to in-house schemes not used in any other library. Both DDC and LC are constructed using a hierarchical arrangement working from the general to the more specific.

Dewey Decimal Classification

In this system, knowledge is divided up using a system based on ten main classes. As more detail of the subject matter is included, the numbers have figures added to them resulting in a number of up to three digits followed by a decimal point and any number of digits. For example, the DDC edition 21 places the medical condition leukaemia at 362.19699419 (medical services emphasis) or 616.99419 (medicine and health emphasis).

The main classes are:

0 Computer science, information and general works
1 Philosophy and psychology
2 Religion
3 Social sciences
4 Language
5 Science
6 Technology
7 Arts and recreation
8 Literature
9 History and geography

These numbers do not operate in the same way as mathematical numbers. For example, the number 42 (four two and not forty-two) will be found further along the sequence from 401 (four zero one, not four hundred and one). When searching for an item, each digit should be taken in turn.

Library of Congress classification

The LC classification scheme is based on the division of subjects into areas using 21 letters of the alphabet:

A General works
B Philosophy, psychology, religion
C Auxiliary sciences of history
D History (general) and history of Europe
E History of America (US)
F History of America (including British, French and Dutch America and Latin America)
G Geography, anthropology, recreation
H Social sciences
J Political science
K Law
L Education
M Music and books on music
N Fine arts
P Language and literature
Q Science
R Medicine
S Agriculture
T Technology
U Military science
V Naval science
Z Bibliography, library science, information resources (general)

Each class is broken down into subclasses such as:

Fine art:

• NA for architecture
• NB for sculpture

At this point, numbers are added for each narrower subject, for example:

- NA 1995 Architecture as a profession
- NA 7100–7884 Domestic architecture. Houses. Dwellings

Variations of classification

Some libraries adapt classification systems to suit their own purposes whilst others have created their own systems. There are systems which have been developed to serve specific subject areas, for example the *British Catalogue of Music Classification* by E. J. Coates, or the *Moys* system of classification for use in law libraries developed by Elizabeth Moys.

The shelfmark of an item may include a suffix as well as the classification number. This may be the first three letters of the author's name or the title and imposes further order, particularly when there are many items at one class number.

Classification numbers may be long, complex and unmemorable, so always have a pencil and paper handy to jot down the numbers of the items required.

Use of separate sequences

A classification system allows the library to shelve all its stock in order starting at the beginning of the sequence until it reaches the end. In practice, this is rarely what happens. Library collections often comprise a number of shorter sequences. These may be a main sequence plus collections of:

- short loan or reference use only items
- audio visual materials
- oversized or folio books shelved together in order to save space
- official publications
- statistics
- special or rare collections
- newspapers

and so on.

The library's catalogue should contain information regarding the physical location, including the sequence in which the item has been shelved. Check carefully, as much time and energy can be wasted looking for an item in the incorrect place.

Special collections

Many libraries have collections that have been acquired over the years and retain some unique feature. It may be, for example, a bequest of a collector of early editions, a collection of books in a particular subject area, ancient and valuable manuscripts, or the works of a particular scholar or author. These special collections are often shelved discretely not within the main collection. They may be closed access when other parts of the library are not. They may also require some additional arrangements for access such as a letter from a home library or used only in a specified area of the building. Find out about any special arrangements before visiting a library and requesting access to any special collections.

Numbers in use around the library

Apart from shelfmarks, there are many other numbering systems in use in a library.

Item number

Classification or call numbers should not be confused with an item number. Libraries usually assign a unique identification number to each individual item. This is a means of identifying one particular copy of a **work**. For example, a library may hold eight copies of the fourth edition of Donald J. Shoemaker's book, *Theories of Delinquency: An Examination of Explanations of Delinquent Behavior*. All the copies will probably have the same classification number. However, they will each have a unique identification number, often a barcode number.

ISBN and ISSN

Most catalogues will include details of a monograph's ISBN (International Standard Book Number) and a serial's ISSN (International Standard Serial Number), a unique number assigned to each title.

ISBN

- varies within the same title with each format (that is, hardback, paperback) and each edition (first and subsequent editions, international student edition and so on)
- a string of 10 digits (the last digit is sometimes replaced by a letter 'x'), for example, 0 099 75181 X

ISSN

- unique for each title
- all issues of a serial publication will have the same ISSN
- comprises two sets of four-digit numbers separated by a hyphen, for example *Advances in Physics* ISSN 0001—8732
- the last digit may be a letter 'x'

If an item does not have an ISBN or ISSN the library will assign a control number of its own to identify the title.

Using a library catalogue

A library catalogue is a list of items which that library stocks, whatever format. Each work has a catalogue record comprising bibliographic (or other) details of the work. Most medium and large libraries have progressed from a card index, via microfiche or other format, to an online public access catalogue, commonly known as an OPAC. The catalogue is the user's key to the library – it provides the mechanism to discover what the library stocks and the status and location of each item. Researchers should ensure they are competent and efficient users of library catalogues, whatever system is used.

Some historic and smaller private collections may have a printed list rather than an OPAC or other electronic database. If the catalogue of an information provider is only available in print, either a copy will have to be obtained or a visit made to the collection in order to view the catalogue.

The OPAC

Web OPACs can be accessed from anywhere with Internet access. It is customary to allow open access to such OPACs, that is, without the need for a password. Although this does not guarantee a user's right to access the materials held in the library, it is a vital discovery tool.

OPACs, although invaluable, are not able to perform the refined searches of the bibliographic databases (see Chapter 6). This means that there are limits to their ability to provide information and it is important to be aware of these restrictions. The information stored on the OPAC is dependent on the quality of the **catalogue record**.

The information contained on the OPAC

The following information may be found using an OPAC:

- a bibliographic (or otherwise) description of the item
- numbers of copies
- location of items
- status of items (for example, on loan to another user, on order and not yet in stock)
- details of serial holdings
- personal borrower record
- reading list information, that is, details of the reading list on which an item appears, the name of the lecturer plus access to that lecturer's complete lists

The OPACs of specialist libraries such as that at the Chetham's Library[6] may also include information such as:

- binding information
- details of provenance and ownership for items of historical interest
- details of others associated with the item, such as printers and booksellers

Linking to full text of e-resources

Online catalogues are useful for linking to electronic formats. A member of a library can often navigate easily from the catalogue to the full text of electronic works. Users will only be able to access these resources:

- if they are entitled to
- if they have the appropriate username and password where required

The holdings of a print and electronic version of a publication may vary. Users should check the electronic holdings as they would the print version.

What is a catalogue record?

A catalogue record is a description of a work. There are standard details that should appear in a properly constructed record that allow the user to identify and locate a particular work using a number of entry points (such as the author).

The information a catalogue record contains

A catalogue record for a book may include details of:

- the author
- the title of the work
- the edition number
- details of publication
- physical description (size, number of pages, and so on)
- series information

- notes (for example, 'previous edition 1989')
- shelfmark and ISBN

The record may be constructed to ease discovery by the user. Therefore it may include information such as additional authors or an alternative spelling of the author's name. It may contain subject headings assigned to the item (see below).

Subject access

The subject headings included in a catalogue record may come from an approved list which ensures consistency (both within one library and between different libraries), for example the Library of Congress Subject Headings (LCSH) which are becoming an international standard and are included in British Library catalogue records. Another widely adopted system of subject headings is the MeSH (Medical Subject Headings) thesaurus developed by the National Medical Library in the US. Users can take advantage of the controlled vocabulary to search for items in the subject they require. Specialist libraries may include additional information such as terms from the Rare Books and Manuscripts Section (RBMS) of the ACRL (Association of College and Research Libraries). In addition, authority files are created so that works by authors with the same name are not confused.

Universal bibliographic records

Although an ideal world is one where every publication, be it a book, leaflet or Web site, has a perfect bibliographic description attached to it, this is not the reality. Most **ephemeral** publications and **grey literature** do not have any record associated with them at the point of publication. For this reason it can be difficult to locate these items.

Searching the library catalogue

Good catalogue records provide the user with a number of entry points depending on the information they have available. The user may know the full details of the item they wish to access, they may want to find out what the library stocks in a particular subject area or may want to find a number of books by the same author. Be aware of the different search options so that the most appropriate can be selected, resulting in efficient and effective searching of the catalogue. As with all searching, check the help available to find the most effective means of searching. There may be advice on phrase searching, on the use of **stopwords**, default settings and other help (see Chapter 7).

Selecting the appropriate catalogue

Although many large libraries have a single catalogue where all their stock is listed, small and specialist libraries may offer a number of different catalogues. For example, the London Library[7] currently has three catalogues:

- the Online Computer Catalogue – for the majority of material acquired since 1950
- the Printed and Card Catalogues – for material acquired before 1950 and items not yet on the online catalogue acquired between 1950 and 1983

Anyone using this library would have to note that the catalogues are defined by the date the material was acquired by the library, not when it was published. This library is running a major project to transfer all its records to the online catalogue; expected completion date is 2009.

In addition to the main catalogue, libraries may have sub-catalogues which allow the user to limit their search to, for example journals or audio visual materials. This is a valuable tool for reducing the numbers of irrelevant results. The British Library[8] allows options to search for items that are reference use only or that are available via document supply services.

Catalogues may or may not include details of other resources, for example:

- electronic resources: may be on a separate list or Web page
- artefacts may not be included

Searching by author

An author search option usually allows the use of an editor's name. An unusual family name (or surname) can be searched for on its own resulting in a manageable number of results. Searching using a common name is less successful. The search can be narrowed down using the author's initials or first name, but be aware that the catalogue record will contain the author's name as it appears in the item. For a single author, this may vary from record to record, for example:

- Lawrence, D. H.
- Lawrence, David Herbert
- Lawrence, David
- Lawrence, D.
- Lawrence, David H.

This example using the British Library Public Catalogue (reference material only) produces the results shown in Table 2.1.

Table 2.1 Example of a search using an author's name

Search term (author field)	Numbers of hits
Lawrence	15,095
Lawrence, D. H.	311
Lawrence, David	620
Lawrence, David Herbert	544
Lawrence, D.	472
Lawrence, David H.	0

Source: British Library Public Catalogue (reference material only), 19 January 2004

There is always the possibility that there is some error in the spelling of the author's name resulting from:

- incorrect details given to the searcher
- a name that has a homonym, such as Pierce/Pearce
- a foreign name that may be spelt in different ways in English transliteration such as Tchaikovsky/Tchaikowsky/Chaikovsky

- a typographical error on the part of the searcher
- a double-barrelled or other hyphenated name (for example, Al-Amin)
- an error on the part of the cataloguer

A Web-based catalogue may include the author name as a link. Clicking on the link will retrieve other records of works by the same author.

Searching by keyword

This method of searching looks for words anywhere in the record or only in the title, depending on the catalogue. Between one and four words should be selected to act as keywords. The more uncommon the word(s), the fewer results will be retrieved. Keyword searching may be used to search for a particular item or as a form of subject search. If the keyword search looks for words only in the title, items on a similar topic that do not have the chosen word(s) in the title will not be retrieved. If the default setting of the search facility is 'AND' the addition of more keywords will narrow the search (see Chapter 7). If a term is included in the title of an item, the item is likely to be relevant.

Some catalogues automatically incorporate plurals and alternative spellings in the search: check before searching.

Searching by author/keyword

When the user knows the publication they wish to retrieve, the author/keyword option can be a reliable method of retrieval. This combination of two fields is useful for listing items by a single author on a particular topic, allowing the discovery of other works by the same author in the same area, although the caveats for keyword and author searching given above still apply.

Searching by title

A title search allows the users to be specific regarding the item they wish to retrieve, but the drawback can be that, unless the search **query** is identical to the title in the catalogue record, the item will not be retrieved. Searching using the first three or four words from the title will often suffice. Some catalogues have the title/keyword search field combined. The British Library Public Catalogue and the COPAC[9] (CURL – Consortium of University Research Libraries – OPAC) union catalogue title search fields accept keywords from the title.

Subject searching

A comprehensive subject search depends on records including reliable subject information. There may be differences in the subject headings used. For example, one item may use LCSH and another a different set of terms. This type of search is useful for retrieving records that are about a similar topic, but which do not necessarily include the chosen term as a word in the title.

A Web-based catalogue may include subject headings as links. Clicking on the link will retrieve other records with the same heading as can be seen when using the University of Oxford's union catalogue, OLIS.

Classification searching

Classification searching is useful for retrieving the records of items shelved at the same classification number and therefore probably containing similar subject matter. It will not retrieve items on a similar subject classified at a different number.

IBSN/ISSN searching

This type of search will retrieve exact matches and records may not be linked. For example, a search using the ISBN 0335193978 will retrieve a record for the paperback edition of Orna and Stevens' book *Managing Information for Research* (Orna 2000) if the library has a record for this edition of the book. It will only retrieve the record for the hardback version (ISBN 0335193986) if the numbers have been linked in some way. If the records are not linked, the library may hold a copy of the book the user requires, but does not retrieve details from the catalogue. The same is true of different editions of titles.

Limiting the search

Some catalogues allow for the setting of limits to a search so that the user can be more prescriptive. Limits may include:

- selecting a specific location
- searching a sub-catalogue (see above)
- date of publication (a specified year or range of years)
- details of the publisher
- language

Spelling, abbreviations, punctuation

See Chapter 7.

Other information or services available on the catalogue

Library catalogues vary with the functions that they offer users. Some of the more common functions are explained below.

Further information about the title

The information that is displayed on the screen is not always the full details of the work held on the catalogue. There may be an option to reveal other details such as the full record.

Loan type

Many libraries use a number of different loan types, for example ordinary (or long) loan, short loan or desk loan (whilst some items will be reference use only). Check this information on the catalogue, as the different loan types may be shelved in various locations.

Numbers of copies

The user can determine the numbers of copies of a work held by the library and how many are available for loan.

Due date

If an item is out on loan, the date when the item is due for return is given. This can determine whether or not the user considers it worthwhile placing a reservation on the item (see below).

Reservations/held items

An OPAC will usually allow a user to place a reservation on an item and discover how many reservations are already placed by others. They may find out if another user has reserved an item that they themselves have on loan (the consequence of this may be that the user is not permitted to renew the item). The user may be able to request that the library holds the item for them to collect later, although not all libraries offer this service.

Status: on order/missing/withdrawn

Other status information may be:

- on order: the library has placed an order for the work and is awaiting its arrival
- missing: the library previously held a copy of the item, but it has gone astray
- withdrawn/deleted: the library previously held a copy of the item, but it has been withdrawn (this could be for a number of reasons, such as bad state of repair, copies removed to make additional space for new editions, and so on)

ILL requests

Some libraries run a system via their OPAC that allow eligible users to request items via interlibrary loan. A signed copyright agreement will have to be supplied.

The personal borrower record

Members of a library may be able to access their personal borrower record via the OPAC. This allows them to check:

- the items they have out on loan
- the due dates of the items they have out on loan
- whether another individual has placed a reservation on an item they have out on loan
- renewal of loaned items

A personal username and password will probably be required to access the borrower record.

What the user will not find on the catalogue

Extensive though many catalogues are, there is some information not discernible using the catalogue. This includes:

- details of who currently has an item out on loan. Libraries will not give out details of a user to other individuals.
- information such as the book being returned ten minutes ago and awaiting shelving
- the fact that someone has shelved the item in the incorrect place and it cannot be found at its correct shelfmark
- that the item is lying on a photocopier/desk having been used by someone else

And possibly:

- 'in' references, that is, details of individual chapters in a book
- records of individual articles in journals
- individual contents of music CDs/records (that is, the separate tracks)

although some libraries catalogue items to this detail.

Other types of catalogue

This chapter has focused on OPACs, but there are other forms of library catalogue in existence.

Card index

The user has to visit the library in order to access the catalogue. There will usually be at least two indexes: author index and title/ subject index. The index should contain cross references.

Printed catalogue

Users may be able to obtain (either free or for a fee) a copy of a printed index. This type of catalogue may become quickly out of date.

Microfiche

The user probably has to visit the library to access the catalogue. The currency depends on how frequently the microfiches are reprinted.

Bibliography

Some small libraries such as the Armitt Library in Cumbria do not possess a library catalogue, but produce a bibliography with some details of the items held by the library.

Key points

- Spend time becoming familiar with the library, its layout, resources, services and the staff who are able to offer help
- Learn how to use the library catalogue effectively

● 3

FORMATS OF INFORMATION SOURCES

Chapter outline

- Introduction
- Issues under consideration
- Print/hard copy (text based)
- Electronic (not including audio and visual materials)
- Audio visual formats
- Artefacts
- People

Introduction

The format of material is the storage medium in which information or data is retained. Even before the onset of electronic storage, there was a plethora of formats for storing information. One could go back as far as clay tablets and papyrus, but this book concerns itself with the common formats encountered by researchers in the twenty-first century and issues associated with each. Many documents are available in multiple formats, for example a journal such as the *Official Journal of the European Union* is available in print, on the Internet and on CD-ROM (EU 2004).

The formats included in this chapter are:

- print (text-based and including manuscripts and incunabula, microforms, maps and atlases)
- electronic (not including audio and visual materials)
- audio visual formats (audio; image; moving image)
- artefacts

Issues under consideration

Researchers will be familiar with the most common formats in which information and data are stored such as the print versions of books and journals. Those with specialist interests will be familiar with using formats such as music recordings, images and maps. Depending on the subject area, be prepared to find information in many different formats, some of more recent development than others. Each is examined using some or all of the following criteria:

- currency
- ease of use
- accessibility
- ease of searching the content
- bibliographic records/description
- longevity
- price
- the role of the publisher

It becomes clear when using criteria such as those above, why some formats have existed as long as they have. And given this tested longevity, it can be explained why archivists are not willing to adopt modern alternatives for long-term storage without their proven success.

Print/hard copy (text based)

Monographs

A monograph is a publication that is complete in itself or forms part of a finite number of parts. Depending on the content, the publisher and the dedication of the author(s), it may take around 18 months for a book to move from conception or proposal to the supplier's shelves. During this period, the content may have dated or have been superseded and authors have to be particularly careful when including information such as URLs (Universal Resource Locators) and screenshots of electronic sources which could easily prove redundant when the book is published.

There has been much talk of the death of the book. This is unlikely given people's unwillingness to read long documents from a screen, coupled with the convenient, portable nature of a book. Books will continue to be a viable format, although scholarly authors may prefer to take advantage of the features of an electronic format for certain publications (see e-books, Chapters 11 and 17). A book that is currently in print and for which the user has the bibliographic details should be relatively easy to obtain. Problems can arise with books that are no longer in print, particularly if they are antique or rare. On the other hand, book details are often released prior to publication and researchers may be left waiting with the promise of a book, only to discover many months later that publication has been abandoned.

Foreign language titles may cause some difficulty: recourse to a specialist book supplier might prove successful. If the bibliographic details are sketchy, one can refer to the catalogue of a foreign national library or a publisher's Web site. The Internet has been a boon in this area as a search can be run which often results in useful details of the publication or holdings in some corner of the world.

Researchers should check for new editions of books that have been in print for a few years. Successful titles will often be revised or updated. If a previous edition is required, obtaining such titles can be difficult. Some titles go out of print surprisingly quickly when publishers commit to small print runs.

Print on demand may be a means of keeping titles, especially those with a small readership, permanently in print. It is a convenient method of allowing access to back lists or titles that would previously have been deemed out of print. At the present time, it is not common, although online commercial booksellers are including print on demand titles in their current lists. This facility may increase in popularity providing customers are happy to download large documents or if publishers adopt the technology to produce books in this way. Another alternative that may develop is that of customers being given the option to purchase a section of a book via print on demand rather than the entire item.

The traditional search facility of a monograph is that of the index. A well-constructed index enables the reader to locate topics of interest within the text. Obviously the index cannot list every word and phrase in the text (although see the section on e-books below) and its use requires some skill on the part of the reader to refer to suitable terms.

Monographs by established publishers usually have a bibliographic description provided by a national library. These descriptions allow for reliable cataloguing and therefore easy search and retrieval. Problems of a lack of bibliographic descriptions occur with grey literature and ephemera (works not published by the common commercial means) and can result in the item being difficult to discover and obtain.

Printed materials have a proven record of longevity providing they are properly stored and curated. Hardback publications are more robust than paperback or flimsy products, but all can last for long periods of time. Those wishing to access rare historical items will be expected to take the proper precautions such as the use of a suitable book rest or the wearing of gloves.

In general, the publisher takes the risk when publishing a work and will assess the market, as well as obtaining reviews of the content of a title prior to publication. Some titles are published by the author and such titles will not have been through the review process. Readers should therefore be aware of a work's pedigree.

Monographs may include: textbooks; novels; scholarly works; encyclopaedias; dictionaries; Festschrift (published in honour of a scholar); handbooks.

Serial publications

The term serial as defined by Hawkins and Hirons from the Library of Congress refers to 'a continuing resource issued in a succession of discrete parts, usually bearing numbering, that has no predetermined conclusion. Examples of serials include journals, magazines, electronic journals, continuing directories, annual reports, newspapers, and monographic series' (Hawkins and Hirons 2002).

A serial publication usually contains more recent material than that in monographs: it may be a matter of months between conception and publication. Even so, the researcher should be aware of this time lag. Daily newspapers, however, take only a single day (or even less) before publication.

Accessibility to printed serials is variable. Whilst many of the major journals in a particular subject area may be stocked by a researcher's home library, access to more obscure and foreign language titles and back runs may be more difficult. It is often the case in libraries that particular titles or even particular issues are more accessed than others and these items quickly become worn. Like any printed item, they are open to abuse and vandalism and many a researcher has despaired at the missing copy. Problems such as this can usually be rectified, but inconvenience the user.

Individual copies are given a number or date and may be gathered together to form volumes. Libraries send bundles of individual issues that form a whole volume for binding into a single hardback item. This is a disruptive process as the copies will be absent from the library for some time.

Many periodical publications provide a printed index to their contents, often at the end of the volume or calendar year. As with monographs, the usefulness of the index relies on the skills of both the indexer and the user. There may be a cumulative index that covers all volumes. Most online databases incorporate the details of print titles in their contents, and are a means of searching for bibliographic details. Most academic journals require an **abstract** of each article. Sometimes these abstracts are published separately.

Serial publications sometimes change their title. This can lead to confusion when accessing a title as the user may be unsure as to whether or not they are referring to the correct title. It is common to encounter abbreviations for serial titles. To ascertain the full title, use a publication such as *Periodical Title Abbreviations*, a three-volume work with entries listed by abbreviation and title (Alkire 2003) or an online source such as *Journal Abbreviation Sources* (McKiernan 2003).

The cost of subscription to academic journals is currently the subject of heated discussion between publishers, libraries and academics. The price of subscription typically rises higher than the rate of inflation and this has an impact on library budgets (see Chapter 17). The cost of subscription to an individual is usually less than that of an institution.

Many academic journals are peer reviewed. This process involves submitted articles being sent out to subject specialists for comment prior to publication. It is this process that enables readers to have faith in the academic reliability of an article. Researchers should be aware whether or not the journals they use are peer reviewed, and this should be taken into account in their evaluation of the validity of the content.

Conference papers

Publications relating to a conference, convention or symposium may include pre-prints, proceedings and conference records. These publications can be called grey literature (see below).

Pre-prints are often published before or in time for the event and can be a valuable record of work currently in progress. The papers are reviewed following the event and published as conference proceedings or transactions. Because conference speakers deliver papers concerning their current work, they are a vital resource for researchers wishing to remain up to date with activities in their chosen subject area. Depending on the organization arranging the conference, proceedings may be made available shortly after the event and easy to access. Sadly, this is not always the case as some papers are not published until a long period has lapsed and others are only available at the event itself.

Because of these problems and the fact that no bibliographic records may exist, conference papers can be difficult to obtain.

The publisher is often a professional body such as the IEEE (Institute of Electrical and Electronics Engineers), the AES (Audio Engineering Society), the BMA (British Medical Association) or the Royal Historical Society and not a large publishing house.

Searching conference proceedings is made possible by indexes such as the *Conference Papers Index* (provided by Cambridge Scientific Abstracts), *Index to Scientific and Technical Proceedings* (from ISI Web of Knowledge) and the British Library's *Zetoc*[1] service. Many of the indexes are published electronically. Details of the author and title of a paper can sometimes be found by seeking out the conference Web site.

Manuscripts and incunabula

Manuscripts can include items such as letters, manuscripts of poems and novels, notebooks and diaries. Incunabula are early printed books, generally prior to the sixteenth century. All of these items may be difficult to trace and access. The British Library has an early printed collection and an incunabula short title catalogue (ISTC) which includes locations from around the world. The key to finding these items can be to identify collections which contain holdings in a relevant subject area. Because of their nature, access may be restricted. Collections that hold such materials will probably include archives, private collections, collections of learned societies and so on (see Archives, Chapter 11).

Grey literature and ephemera

Grey literature comprises those publications that are not easily identified nor accessed via the usual sources such as booksellers. Types of grey literature include:

- conference proceedings (see above)
- theses
- company reports
- some official publications

- research papers prior to publication
- local records

These types of publications do not usually have a linked bibliographic description nor an ISBN and this lack of information
means that they can be difficult to obtain.

Ephemera are those publications which are often disposable or
single sheets that would not be considered minor publications.
The *Concise Oxford Dictionary* defines the word ephemeral as
'lasting or of use for only a short time; transitory' (Allen 1991:
393). Because of this there are difficulties in both identifying and
accessing these materials. Although not scholarly documents,
they can form a vital part of a researcher's information resources.
Ephemera may include:

- pamphlets
- leaflets such as marketing or promotional materials
- forms

There are often no records that they have been produced at all,
especially in the public domain. Ephemeral publications may be a
'one-off' with no remaining copies.

In more recent years, libraries have become aware of the lack of
information and holdings of these materials and a number of
projects and bodies such as SIGLE[2] (System for Information on
Grey Literature in Europe) have been set up to attempt to document and retain holdings.

Publishers of these documents may be anyone from a large
organization, a government body, a commercial company or an
individual. The majority of ephemeral documents may be lost.
Many are supplied free of charge whilst some may only be
available internally to members of an organization.

Maps and charts

The range of maps and charts is vast and libraries may be selective
about the collection they retain. Storage can be difficult: large
maps require large flat drawers, atlases can be oversized and

difficult to handle and historical maps may need special archival conditions. Currency can be imperative in certain situations, but historical data is of equal value in others.

Maps can be made using a variety of criteria and the researcher may need to consider any or all of the following variables:

- date
- scale
- topographical subject matter
- geological subject matter
- land use subject matter
- atlases (road atlas, demographic, historical and so on)
- whether or not the map was created by a national survey organization

Difficulties might be encountered when attempting to locate and access foreign and historical maps. Atlases may contain an index which guides the searcher to particular page and map reference, but maps do not usually have this information.

Cataloguers should follow the guidelines for cartographic materials, but this is dependent on the skill of the cataloguer. Researchers should be prepared for some lateral thinking when searching catalogues for maps and charts.

Maps may be produced by a national survey organization such as the Ordnance Survey (Ordnance Survey 2004) in the UK, specialist institutes such as the British Geological Society or commercial publishers, then stored in specialist libraries such as that at the Royal Geographical Society[3]. They are increasingly being made available in a digital format (for example by the British Geological Survey[4]) and users should be aware of different data storage, for example raster images and vector data and whether specialist software such as a GIS (Geographical Information System) is required. Specialist maps may be expensive.

Microforms

- Microfilm, microfiche and microprint (and microcard) are all types of microform. Each is a means of storing an image of a document in a reduced version.

- Microfiche is a 15 cm by 10 cm (6 inches by 4 inches) sheet of film that can hold up to about 100 pages at 24-times reduction
- Microfilm comes in two sizes: 16 mm and 35 mm
- Microprint (and microcard) is less common. The image is stored on a stiff card.

Microstorage formats are relatively cheap to produce and are expected to be long-lasting, so are still a popular choice for documents such as rare items which should not be handled, those in a bad state of repair and those with a limited print run. Because of the low cost, they are sometimes used for indexes and other records that need to be kept up to date and therefore frequently produced. An additional benefit for the library or organization is that of storage: microforms take up very little space.

All these forms necessitate the use of a special reader to enable the user to view the information. Many libraries possess a microfilm/fiche/print reader and some also have the extra facility of a reader/printer for printing copies of the document(s). Like photocopying, there is likely to be a charge for this service. These machines are straightforward to operate, although it can be a challenge loading a microfilm in the correct orientation if a previous user has wound the film on the spool incorrectly. As with computer visual display units (VDUs), it is difficult to read large amounts of material on a screen. Because they are an image rather than computer-readable data, searching involves use of an index (if it exists).

Items that are likely to be stored in microform are:

- newspapers (for example, the British Library Newspaper collection)
- books (the Library of Congress[5] has a large collection)
- rare or historic documents (for example, medieval manuscripts, author's original manuscripts, notebooks or correspondence)
- indexes and bibliographies
- historical records or historical and genealogical society information
- many other primary sources of information (for example, parliamentary papers and cabinet minutes)

- theses and **dissertation**s (as held by the British Library Document Supply Centre)

Although many libraries house microform collections, users need to be aware of how these items are indicated on the catalogue. The RLSG (Research Support Libraries Group) ran a survey of microforms in UK HE institutions. They concluded that 'it is clear from this survey that records for these kinds of material are imperfect and inconsistent. As a class they can not uniformly be retrieved through OPACs' (Feather 1999: 17).

Many research libraries hold microforms and corresponding readers. The British Library and the Library of Congress have extensive collections of microform materials.

Electronic (not including audio and visual materials)

The general electronic formats referred to here include:

- Web-based/online resources
- CD-ROMs
- formats such as PDF (Portable Document Format), word processing, spreadsheets and databases
- floppy disk
- electronic versions of print formats (for example, e-journals)

Electronic formats of information sources have a number of benefits:

- they can be kept up to date, sometimes to the hour (for example, legal databases such as *Westlaw* from Sweet and Maxwell are updated three times per day so that users have access to the most recent information)
- many can be accessed from anywhere in the world with suitable equipment and authentication
- flexible searching of content
- they do not take up any physical storage space (apart from the necessary hardware)
- additional data, multimedia sources and appropriate Web sites can be accessed directly from the content via a link

However, the situation is not always as rosy as it may at first seem. Internet-based resources can be current, but this relies on the publisher updating regularly. If a problem with currency is identified, the user may lose faith in its reliability. CD-ROMs may only be updated monthly, or even quarterly. They are therefore not always particularly current, especially towards the end of the current period.

Many electronic formats are designed to be intuitive and easy to use, even for the unfamiliar user. Interfaces vary from those that guide the user step by step, to those that are complex for the new user. There are sometimes confusing quirks regarding usage. A member of library staff will help in the use of electronic resources.

The accessibility of electronic resources is dependent on three factors:

- authentication and authorization
- location (for IP (Internet protocol) authentication)
- hardware and software

Although some electronic resources are freely available (for example, services such as BUBL[6], the Bulletin Board for Libraries (full name no longer used) or the RDN[7] (Resource Discovery Network)), others require authentication, usually in the form of a username and password. Without the appropriate authentication, the user is unable to access the resource (see Chapter 2). An Internet-based resource is often available from anywhere in the world with Internet access. Those that restrict use by using IP address as authentication will only be available from computers having those addresses. Often CD-ROM resources are only available on a network in a particular location.

One of the real benefits of electronic resources is the ability to search the entire content. The success of this depends on the skill of the user and the construction of the resource. Some resources offer only a basic search facility whilst others allow for detailed, structured searching. Users should be aware of the maxim 'rubbish in, rubbish out,' and search with care.

As with hardcopy materials, the bibliographic records of electronic resources vary. Users often experience difficulties when attempting to reference electronic sources (see Chapter 13): this is a result of them being unsure which information needs to be included and/or a lack of the information required.

Electronic formats such as CD-ROMs and DVDs have not been in existence long enough to prove their longevity. Since CDs only came on the market in 1982, it has yet to be proven whether or not they will retain all the data stored on them in a readable form for long-term storage. Another major problem is that of retaining the hardware or the programs to be able to read the files. It is likely that DVD format will be superseded by another format not yet invented. Libraries often retain copies of resources in a format on which they believe they can rely, which may explain why microform is still going strong.

Audio visual formats

Since Thomas Edison applied for the patent of his wax phonograph in 1877 there have been a host of developments in the devices designed to store audio. The same is true of the means of recording and storing images, both still and moving. A huge leap was made with the dawn of the digital era. This gave rise to many of the devices that are in common use today.

Currency is not generally an issue in audio visual recordings as they are usually the record of an event or performance at a specific point in time or of a work of art.

Audio visual items often form specialist collections, for example the National Sound Archive (at the British Library). As is the case with printed items, rare and historic items can be difficult to obtain or access.

The search facility of audio or moving image recordings can be a problem. If a modern recording has some form of timecode built in which the searcher is able to use, and they know the point they wish to access, all is well and good. A score may aid a search of a music recording, but other than that, it relies on the searcher's knowledge and patience. Still images may form part of a volume with an index which can be used to locate a particular image.

Provided adequate care is taken, the lifespan of a vinyl disc, film or photograph may be extremely long (although there has not been the opportunity to test these formats over more than a century or so). As with other electronic resources, the case of digital recordings is as yet unknown. And similarly, reproduction relies on suitable equipment being available.

Some of the older formats may be transferred to a more modern system (for example, a cinefilm may be transferred to video or DVD). If this is the case, the modern format may be easily accessible and the original remain in ideal conditions in an archive.

The cost of these items is the price charged for obtaining a copy. For example, the National Sound Archive charges by the hour (copies are made in real time), ranging from £40 for an individual user to £165 for commercial use. Quality diminishes with each subsequent copy made, although modern transcription techniques make this less of a problem. Any copies made by the researcher should comply with current copyright law.

The publisher of an audio visual item may not always be obvious. Commercial recordings have the identity of the publisher on the packaging and/or the item itself, but identification of the publisher of an obscure item may present problems.

A library stocking any audio visual formats may also provide the means for playing them. A user might be able to manipulate the controls expertly on a MP3 player, but not be so confident in how to operate a reel-to-reel tape recorder or vinyl disc player. There should be a member of staff available to help the user in use of equipment.

A single item, such as a CD or vinyl disc may contain the recordings of a number of works. The full contents are not always included in the catalogue record, so a searcher looking for a recording of the *Chopin Fantaisie-Impromptu Opus 66* may not discover a recording on a disc with the title *Great Pianists of the 20th Century: Artur Rubenstein* (Rubinstein 1998).

Artefacts

An artefact could be almost anything and libraries may contain a selection, although some items are more likely to be housed in a museum. The researcher in pursuit of artefacts will need to search for the details to locate the item, for example in a museum or library catalogue. The catalogue records should contain descriptive information and may contain a photograph of the item.

Artefacts can include a vast array of forms such as:

- specimens (geological, medical and so on)
- toys
- tools
- teaching materials (for example, those used in an infant school)

Researchers may need to obtain special permission to access and handle items and it is likely they will have to travel to the library or museum.

People

One must not overlook this valuable form of information storage. Whether it is an expert in the chosen subject, a colleague or members of the public, researchers often tap into the knowledge (or opinions) of others. Eliciting information may take care and persistence and the researcher will need some form of storage for the information gathered. This could be in the form of an audio recording, notes taken during an interview, a questionnaire and so on.

Key points

- Be familiar with the benefits and drawbacks of the formats used
- Be aware of the difficulties of accessing some formats and plan the research accordingly

---

4

FINDING INFORMATION ABOUT EXISTING RESEARCH

Chapter outline

- The type of research referred to in this chapter
- Access to information about research
- Indexes and online databases of research activity
- Research Councils UK and other bodies
- Theses

The type of research referred to in this chapter

The research with which this chapter deals is that which is undertaken in academic institutions and/or funded by a major research funding body such as one of the UK Research Councils. Other research may be that which is ongoing in commercial companies or registered charities. One of the problems with much research activity is that the publications associated with it are not formally published and may not be available via commercial channels (grey literature: see Chapters 3 and 11).

This chapter is concerned solely with publications and sources that give bibliographic details of research as opposed to the full text of research papers and other scholarly documents (see Chapter 11). Another means of finding information about research is by citation searching (see Chapter 8).

Access to information about research

Details of research can be difficult to obtain and perhaps may not be in the public domain. The reasons for this may be:

- it is restricted company information (for example, information about new products)
- it contains sensitive information (for example, about an individual)
- it may be considered to have legal implications
- it may not have been published using the normal channels

Details can be found in scholarly publications such as published theses, journal articles, conference papers, pre-prints or reports. There are indexes and directories available to aid the discovery of research activity. Some sources rely on the researchers themselves submitting details. This assumes that they are a) aware of the index and b) wish to have details made public. Others are maintained by institutions such as a research library and some obtain information directly from institutions.

Anyone undertaking doctoral or other high-level research must first be sure that what they intend doing is original. They will wish to find out about other research activity in the subject area in order to inform their own work. From an information-seeking perspective, this is an interesting area to monitor for developments (see Chapters 11 and 17). There are initiatives around the world attempting to make research data and records more accessible. Some are national projects whilst others have been set up by individuals or commercial companies. The Web has enabled information about research to be potentially available to anyone with Internet access. However, there is neither a co-ordinated global index nor any national index that can be described as comprehensive.

Indexes and online databases of research activity

Commonwealth Universities Yearbook

This is an annual publication from the ACU (Association of Commonwealth Universities) (Elmes 2003) of over 35,000 entries. It includes information about research centres, institutional data and contact details and its coverage is around 700 universities in 36 countries throughout the Commonwealth. There are staff lists for each university including research staff and directors of research and summaries of main research areas for each department.

Community of Science (COS)

The COS[1] is a Web network that offers services to researchers such as profiles of other researchers (those that have submitted their records) and research institutions, an up to date record of funding opportunities and information about conferences. Institutions, corporations and individuals can join the COS. Its success is dependent on the building of the community by the contributors. Subscribers can search for details of researchers (via the COS Expertise database) and research projects (via the COS Funded Research database). These databases can be searched by keyword, geography, institutional recipient, award amount, date, agency, investigator, departments, and other options.

There are many hundreds of thousands of scientists and scholars who are members of the COS, along with hundreds of universities, research institutions, corporations, businesses and government agencies, around the world. The COS wishes to expand and include details of members in the fields of science, social science and the humanities.

CORDIS (Community Research and Development Information Service)

CORDIS[2] is the research and development gateway of the European Union (EU) which provides information about EU-funded research. It includes details of current and past projects, results and publications via the Research and Technical Development (RTD) publications database. This database, accessible via the CORDIS Web site, holds records of publications from 1962. The research is undertaken by bodies such as commercial organizations, research institutes or universities. Records contain bibliographic information and an abstract. The service offers advanced and professional search facilities for which the user may obtain free access, but must first register.

CORDIS offers opportunities to search for news about breakthroughs in EU research, the Technology Marketplace facilitates access to latest research results and the CORDIS library allows the downloading of research and development documents, conference papers, project reports and other publications.

EAGLE and SIGLE

EAGLE[3] (European Association for Grey Literature Exploitation) manages and provides access to the multidisciplinary SIGLE (System for Information on Grey Literature in Europe) database of European grey literature. SIGLE contains over 800,000 records of information about documents such as technical or research reports, pre-prints, patents, committee reports, working papers, conference papers, discussion and policy papers, government reports and market surveys. The information includes bibliographic details, and records are classified by subject category. Some records include an abstract and all contain information regarding the availability of the document (see Chapter 11). Searching is possible by subject (using the SIGLE classification scheme), report number, issuing organization, author or document type. The content is reliant on information gathered and submitted by the member countries and their representatives. The database is not, however, free.

Sites that subscribe to SIGLE are also permitted access to a number of additional databases such as the Derwent World Patent Index and SOLIS (Social Sciences Literatures Information System). STN International[4] which provides SIGLE has an A–Z facility to search for relevant databases not included in SIGLE and which may be of use to researchers.

Current Legal Research Topics Database project

An interesting development is the provision of the Current Legal Research Topics Database at the IALS (Institute of Advance Legal Studies, University of London). The database is designed to provide a 'comprehensive listing of legal research currently undertaken in British law schools at MPhil (Master of Philosophy) or PhD (Doctor of Philosophy) level' (IALS 2002) and is aimed at postgraduate students and their research supervisors. It gives a brief record, with no contact details, but provides a useful service for those wishing to find current titles.

Other databases

There are a number of online databases of research publications such as *PhD Data*[5]. These are variable in their content and search facilities and some do not show their provenance or ownership. Although they can be a useful resource for finding out about research activity, users should be aware that i) they may run on a commercial basis and ii) entries are submitted by the authors with no verification.

Emerald Research Register

The *Emerald Research Register*[6] is an example of a commercial organization providing an online forum for the dissemination of research to subscribers. The register relies on researchers submitting details themselves. The subject coverage is that of management and related fields. It gives details of start and completion dates and the status of the research, that is, whether it is completed and published or not published, ongoing, not yet commenced or on hold. There are details of contacts, methodologies (from a selection of options) and funding information.

Research Councils UK and other bodies

The research councils

'Research Councils UK (RCUK) is a strategic partnership set up to champion science, engineering and technology supported by the seven UK Research Councils' (RCUK 2004). The councils fund research projects whose details are available via the RCUK. Users may search across the research councils' databases using the Science and Engineering Knowledge Network (SEKNet) which gives brief details of current or recently funded research.

The seven research councils are listed below and each publishes information about the research it has funded. Some maintain databases of research activities.

- BBSRC: the Biotechnology and Biological Sciences Research Council. The BBSRC online database of research and publications is named *Oasis*.
- CCLRC: Council for the Central Laboratory of the Research Councils.
- EPSRC: The Engineering and Physical Sciences Research Council. Details are maintained on the *Research Support/Grants on the Web* pages.
- ESRC: Economic and Social Research Council. The council maintains an online database, *Regard*, of ESRC research since 1985.
- MRC: Medical Research Council.
- NERC: Natural Environment Research Council. A database of funded research, with links to many of the projects, is available on the *Grants on the Web* pages.
- PPARC: Particle Physics and Astronomy Research Council. A database of funded research is available on the *Grants on the Web* pages.

The AHRB (Arts and Humanities Research Board) is not currently classified as a Research Council, but this is due to change. The Board is making the transition to the Arts and Humanities Research Council which is planned to be in place by 2005. Like the other research councils, it grants awards to fund research, in subject areas such as the humanities and creative and performing arts.

The HERO[7] Web site provides links to the research councils and information about research activity in the UK.

Other bodies and funding institutions

Other bodies undertaking research include:

- The Davy Faraday Research Laboratory[8] which forms part of the Royal Institution, carries out research in the area of solid-state science especially in the fields of chemistry and physics of complex materials.
- The British Academy[9] sponsors research projects (called Academy Research Projects), in the humanities and social sciences.
- The Royal Academy of Arts[10] supports artists.
- The US National Academies[11] comprises the National Academy of Sciences, the National Research Council, the National Academy of Engineering and the Institute of Medicine. It is required to advise the US on all aspects of science, technology and medicine. It commissions studies and reports from its members and provides an option for searching current projects.
- The NATO (North Atlantic Treaty Organization) Science Programme[12] provides funding for collaboration and cooperation for science programmes and support for research infrastructure development in participating partner countries. The *NATO Science Series* of publications contains the results of work achieved by the NATO Advanced Study Institutes and Advanced Research Workshops. The publications are available commercially from the publishers, Kluwer Academic Publishers and IOS Press, Amsterdam.

- The NATO Research and Technology Organization (RTO) is governed by the Research and Technology Agency (RTA).[13] The RTO is the centre for defence research and technology programmes. Access to information regarding current and previous research is available via the NATO RTO Web site.
- Mannheim University[14] provides links to research institutions and universities concerned with European topics.

University departments

Most universities provide limited information regarding the research currently taking place in their departments. Finding out what is current at each university is difficult without knowing likely sites where research into a specific subject area may be taking place.

Charitable organizations

Charitable organizations often work in tandem with or directly fund research that takes place in HE. Medical charities may work with scientists in research hospitals; other charities run research projects themselves. For larger charities, details of current research projects are usually easy to find using the WWW. For example, the Institute of Cancer Research[15] provides details of current research and bibliographic information about publications (including abstracts) whilst Action Research[16] gives information about current research projects funded by the charity. The Wellcome Trust funds research into improvements in human and animal health. Details of research activity funded by the Trust are listed by academic year.

Theses

Doctoral theses and dissertations

A doctoral thesis is a published work resulting from research that makes a significant and original contribution to the advancement of knowledge. It is awarded by an HE establishment and the successful candidate is entitled to append the letters PhD, or similar, to their name. In the UK these publications are generally called theses, but in the US, dissertations (a word generally reserved for taught postgraduate and undergraduate projects in the UK).

There is a selection of routes for obtaining details of such publications. In the UK, *Index to Theses* (Expert Information 2004) (see below) is the major sources of information. Theses from other nations may be more problematic. *Dissertations Abstracts International* is a publication that lists details and abstracts of theses from the US and other countries (see below). Occasionally, doctoral theses are published commercially and in these cases, there should be a bibliographic record.

Masters dissertations are not indexed in the same way as doctoral theses. This makes identification more difficult. It should be noted that information contained in these publications is not necessarily original research and institutions may retain copies for a limited period.

Index to theses

This index allows the user to search for higher degrees accepted by the universities of Great Britain and Ireland (Expert Information 2004). It relies on the submission of details of works by the universities. It is available both in print and online (by subscription) and can be searched by author, keyword, title or subject. Abstracts are included from 1988. The print version offers coverage from 1950 and the Web edition from 1970 (Volume 21). The time from submission until publication takes around three months.

Dissertation abstracts database

This database, published by the US publisher UMI[17], holds the details of over one million doctoral and masters theses and dissertations. Coverage begins in 1861 and entries from 1980 include an abstract. The emphasis is on US publications. Many titles are available in full text. Access to the information held on the database is via the following publications:

Dissertation Abstracts International (DAI)

DAI comprises three sections: two covering the US in two broad subject areas and the third, other countries.

A: North America – Humanities and social sciences
B: North America – Sciences and engineering
C: Worldwide, covers non-North American materials. It is published quarterly as a separate volume.

Updating occurs monthly and there is an annual cumulative publication. There are two formats: printed and microfiche. Entries from July 1980 contain abstracts as well as a citation.

Comprehensive Dissertation Index (CDI)

A printed multi-volume work that contains citations from 1861. There is a keyword index for greater subject access.

Masters Abstracts International (MAI)

An electronic, bi-monthly publication which contains citations and abstracts of masters dissertations. Coverage is not comprehensive.

American Doctoral Dissertations (ADD)

This annual publication claims to contain citations for virtually all US dissertations for the academic year (both those published by UMI and others) and is therefore more comprehensive than the North American sections of DAI.

ProQuest Digital Dissertations

Digital Dissertations is an online search service for obtaining details of theses and dissertations. It is possible to search the most recent two years of entries of the *Dissertation Abstracts Database* without a subscription. Two other electronic products available from UMI are *Dissertation Abstracts Ondisc* and *Dissertation Abstracts Online*.

The British Library

The British Thesis Service from the British Library recommends that researchers use SIGLE or *Index to Theses* to find details of UK doctoral theses. Brief records are included in the Document Supply Catalogue on the British Library Public Catalogue (BLPC).

Checking individual academic libraries' catalogues

University libraries catalogue the theses that they hold in stock. A search to find publications in this way can be laborious if the researcher has no knowledge of likely sites in a given subject area.

Key points

- Researchers need to find details of current and past research to inform their own work
- Obtaining details may be difficult as much of the corpus is grey literature

---

5

IDENTIFYING THE
INFORMATION NEED

Chapter outline

- Introduction
- Types of sources of information that will be required
- Primary and secondary sources
- Multidisciplinarity and subject overlap
- Defining the area and limits of the research
- What is already known?

Introduction

Before setting out to find information, it is important to have a plan of what is (and is not) needed. Obviously, the researcher cannot include things of which they are not aware, but an initial outline of the requirements can be created using the most basic knowledge. Reading around and talking to others who have some knowledge of the topic are good starting points for getting a feel for the subject (see also Chapter 7). It is helpful to join appropriate mailing lists and alerting services (see Chapter 16) in order to gather relevant information and monitor current activity. As the project continues, the researcher's journey will enable them to add to their knowledge of sources of information. They will also reject sources and items which may at first have seemed vital.

Having set up the mechanisms for obtaining information as given in Chapter 1 and carefully defined the question or problem, the researcher is ready to move on to the next stage of information-gathering process: defining what information is required.

Types of sources of information that will be required

If the researcher is writing a short essay or report, it may be sufficient to access some key books and journal articles and no other documents. It can, however, become rapidly apparent that more might be necessary. A researcher investigating, for example, the status of women in the workplace may want to quote sections from documents that add weight to the discussion such as the *Equal Pay Act 1970* or government statistics of women's earnings during a particular period. Such information can then be used to support an argument or prove the historical context.

Researchers should consider carefully all the information sources relevant to their work (of which they are aware) before embarking on the search. Needs may change as the research progresses: for example, encyclopaedias are useful for an overview at the outset, but later on more specialist and detailed information will be needed. Or the researcher may read conflicting reports of a situation and decide to access the primary information to ascertain which is the more accurate.

The researcher should therefore decide:

1. What formats of information are likely to be required (see Chapter 3)
2. What types of documents within those formats will be needed (for example, the minutes of meetings, dictionaries, parish records, journal articles, videos of a performance)
3. Whether primary and/or secondary sources will be necessary (see below)

Numbers 2 and 3 should be considered together.

Some examples of types of documents or information might be:

- chapters of books
- journal articles
- newspaper articles
- Web sites
- statistics publications
- official government publications
- leaflets
- theses
- conference proceedings
- the general public
- specialists in the subject area
- audio visual materials
- company reports
- standards
- local or national records (for example, council, genealogical or planning records)

There may be issues with some of these publications such as the length of time between data gathering and publication (see Chapter 3).

Primary and secondary sources

Much research demands that the researcher access both primary and secondary sources of information.

A primary source is one that is a record of events as they are first recorded without analysis or commentary. It may be a set of data, such as census statistics, that has been set out in an orderly fashion, but not interpreted. It may be first-hand accounts or direct evidence of an event or item. Original research often requires primary sources. For example:

- a music scholar may return to original manuscripts to clarify exactly what the composer wrote
- a medical researcher may wish to access data about the sub-

jects in a drugs trial to ascertain the effects of that drug
- a researcher investigating an event may wish to read diaries and letters of those involved

A secondary source is one that interprets or analyses an event or phenomenon. It often attempts to describe or explain primary sources. A secondary source such as a textbook may include some primary sources as examples. Examples of the uses of secondary sources might be:

- the music scholar will obtain articles and commentaries on the work in question to gauge the opinions of other scholars
- the medical researcher reads journal articles on the disease in question to find the experiences of others working in the field
- the historical researcher will access texts of other scholars' interpretation of the event

For some types of research it is imperative to access the primary data. These data provide the building blocks upon which all analysis and interpretation is created. The researcher may know that they need to access primary sources before they set out looking for information, even if they are not sure exactly what the item is that they require. If secondary sources are required, they will need to consider the types of resources appropriate for the project.

Multidisciplinarity and subject overlap

Although much work takes place in a single broad subject area, other research involves two or more disciplines. This may be the result of collaboration or a new perspective on a problem. For example, there are researchers working in areas such as psychoacoustics (the partnership of the perception and science of sound), gender issues in the French media (a mixture of sociology and language) or crop science (including the topics of 'plant genetics and physiology, about pests and disease-causing organisms, about the action of chemical pesticides, and about soil science, climatology and nutrient cycling in ecosystems, and natural selection and adaptation' (BBSRC 2003)). There is an increasing emphasis on research at the border between disciplines, especially with developments in new technologies.

On a narrower level, work may overlap between two or more areas in the same basic discipline, for example machine translation and linguistics.

The individual seeking information for research will therefore have to clarify from which angle(s) they are approaching the topic and identify areas where there is any subject overlap. If this is the case, a researcher familiar with information sources in one subject area, may need to use those of another.

Defining the area and limits of the research

Setting boundaries in both breadth and depth of the chosen topic will maintain the research within the defined topic. The researcher should be clear about the area(s) that is/are included, and equally about what will not be included. This can be achieved by setting limits. Doing this will:

- enable decisions on when to stop gathering information
- help to ascertain whether or not information is pertinent
- keep the research focused, therefore avoiding creeping growth of the subject resulting in an unmanageably large project

For example, a researcher concerned with voter apathy in elections may wish to decide:

- which country/ies to investigate (and therefore which to exclude)
- the types of election (political – general, local; other types of election such as trade union)
- whether the research concerns certain age groups or other category of voter (and therefore which will be ignored)
- whether attitudes towards political parties will include all parties, a selected number or be treated as a more general issue
- what to include regarding related factors such as trades unions, career politicians and the influence of the media. Decisions

should be made about which factors will be investigated and which not
- the time factor, that is, setting a range of dates which the research will cover. For example, any elections regardless of date; all elections held during the twentieth century; the 1997 UK General Election.

This is a general example, but illustrates the point that if limits are not set, the research can quickly expand into additional vast areas, resulting in loss of focus and a badly defined research topic. In essence, the researcher is defining what can be considered relevant material.

What is already known?

Whilst deciding what information is needed for the project, the researcher should document relevant sources of which they are already aware. Under the main subject areas or headings, list the sources already known where information may be found. This should include all sources: people (specialists in the field and personal contacts); publications; other sources such as records, audio visual materials and artefacts; organizations and other bodies; relevant sources of information such as indexes, Web sites, bibliographies or online databases. Where appropriate, they may be checked for additional sources, for example, a book chapter may contain a list of references for other linked or related works.

Key points

- Decide whether or not it is likely that the research requires access to primary sources
- Have a clear idea of the types of resources that will be needed
- Find out about the main resources in other disciplines which are relevant for multidisciplinary work
- Define the scope of the research in detail to prevent 'research creep'
- Document what is already known

⬤ 6

RESOURCE DISCOVERY

Chapter outline

- Resource discovery
- What are abstracts and indexes?
- Online bibliographic databases
- Issues relating to online databases
- Catalogues and bibliographies
- Open access journals
- Other sources and types of information
- References and citation searching
- Selecting sources relevant to the subject

Resource discovery

Having identified the information need, obtaining resources for research is a three-stage process:

1. resource discovery – that is, finding out what resources exist in the chosen topic area
2. resource location – finding out where those resources are stored

3   resource access – actually obtaining the item(s)

Information providers, bodies such as the JISC and librarians are working towards seamless online provision where the user discovers a resource and obtains immediate access to the most **appropriate copy**. Although this situation exists in some areas (depending on subscriptions and service providers), it is not universal and it is probably necessary to work through the three steps of the process.

Resource discovery is the process of finding the details (bibliographic or otherwise) of existing resources that are relevant to the chosen topic. There are a number of sources available that enable the researcher to perform this task. In general they comprise abstracts and indexes, catalogues and bibliographies, although there are other sources that can be tapped.

This chapter is concerned with *where* to look to discover resources and discusses the features of online databases. Chapter 7 gives details of *how* to search for resources.

What are abstracts and indexes?

Many journals provide an index to their contents, often published at the end of each year. Cumulative indexes are less common so, although useful, these annual indexes only include a single year's listings of the contents from one title. If no other source were available, the researcher intending to search more widely would be forced to peruse the indexes of all the titles of interest, a highly unsatisfactory method of working. To resolve this situation, there are indexing services which compile indexes covering large numbers of titles. For example, the *British Nursing Index* lists bibliographic information about journal articles from over 300 journals of interest to those in the nursing profession, and the *Legal Journals Index* performs a similar function for law. There are broader publications that cover interdisciplinary subjects, such as the *British Humanities Index* which includes arts, history, economics, political science and so on.

Indexes may provide only the bibliographic details of the articles, whilst abstracting services also include a summary of the article. Confusingly, indexes also sometimes contain abstracts (see, for example, *Index to Theses*). The presence of an abstract enables the researcher to be more discerning in their selection of articles, as they have a better concept of the content.

Abstracting and indexing services usually list the entries by subject, author or title. There may be additional options for searching the contents.

Some collections have been in publication for many years, for example the *Chemical Abstracts Service* (CAS) claims that 'since 1907, [it] has indexed and summarized chemistry-related articles from more than 40,000 scientific journals, in addition to patents, conference proceedings and other documents pertinent to chemistry, life sciences and many other fields' (CAS 2004). This service, which provides abstracts for more than 22 million documents, is also accessible online.

Like *Chemical Abstracts*, many publishers provide an online subscription service because of the superior access and search options. Performing a search using a printed version is time-consuming and can create a complex search trail that the researcher must be diligent in managing. An online service allows the researcher to perform keyword searches within the text of the abstract and to search other fields such as indexing terms (or descriptors), the language of the record and author affiliation. Coupled with this, users can manage their searches and results efficiently and are often able to set up search alerts (see Chapter 16).

Online bibliographic databases

An online bibliographic database is an electronic store of bibliographic information about journal articles and possibly other resources such as book reviews, reports and conference proceedings. Many are available on CD-ROM (and networked in some institutions), but frequently access is arranged via the WWW. A Web-based database can be updated easily and access via the Internet is preferable for users.

Although much valuable information on the WWW can be found using a search engine, most of the valuable information contained in these databases will not be discovered. Subscribers to online databases pay for:

- the well-ordered structure of the database
- the ability to search in a structured fashion
- the specialist content of the database
- the indexing and thesaurus construction

Most of the large printed indexes and abstracting services have an online version either running in tandem with the printed publication, or replacing it completely. Another benefit of the Internet database is that, in many cases, there are additional live links and facilities on the database not possible in a print version of the same publication such as linking seamlessly from references to full text.

Databases are often supplied through an agent such as Bath Information and Data Service (BIDS, a not-for-profit service) or a commercial supplier. Users pay a subscription and are required to sign a licence (usually paid for and signed on their behalf by their institution) (see Chapter 2).

The records held on bibliographic databases

The records held on bibliographic databases contain information similar to that included in printed abstracts and indexes. However, the distinction between those that supply only bibliographic information and abstracts, and those that supply full text is becoming blurred. As agreements and deals are made between publishers, together with work on the Information Environment and open URLS (see Chapter 17), many are providing seamless links to full text at a separate site (see Chapter 11).

A database such as *Ingenta*[1] is one where the user can access the full text of the journals to which their institution has subscribed, but is able to search the database for records, including abstracts, of other works (and can then find the full text via another source). This chapter is concerned with the bibliographic details and abstracts as supplied by these databases. The issue of full text access is dealt with in Chapter 11.

The entry for each item on the database is called a record and each record contains bibliographic information stored in named fields. The fields may include:

- author(s)
- title (of article)
- source (publication where the article was published)
- volume
- issue/part number
- date of publication
- date of addition to database
- abstract
- major descriptors/subject headings
- minor descriptors/subject headings

For example, the record in Figure 6.1 was retrieved using *Sociological Abstracts* produced by CSA (Cambridge Scientific Abstracts).

Each of the fields may be searched and underlined text is linked to other records on the database or to external Internet sites. The bold text shows the search terms used to retrieve the record. The two-letter abbreviation at the start of each field may be used by the searcher to indicate a search in a named field (see below).

Issues relating to online databases

Although the principles of searching structured databases are the same, each has its individual features. Some are simple in that the options for searching are few, but easy to use. Others are more complex but permit targeted search strategies. Even basic features differ and it is advisable to check the features using the 'Help' function. The database is only as good as the information it is given. If the search query is not acceptable to the database, it will produce unsatisfactory or even no results.

TI: Title Class Matters: The Persisting Effects of Contextual Social Class on Individual Voting in Britain, 1964-97

AU: Author Andersen, Robert; Heath, Anthony

AF: Affiliation Dept Sociology, U Oxford, UK

EA: Email Address mail to: [the author's e-mail address is inserted here]

SO: Source European Sociological Review, 2002, 18, 2, June, 125-138

IS: ISSN 0266-7215

CD: CODEN ESOREP

AB: Abstract This paper extends previous work on the changing importance of individual & contextual social class in GB. We adopt a multilevel framework for analysis, linking surveys from the 1964-1997 British **Election** Studies with Census data on the social-class composition of constituencies. The goal of the paper is to test whether, net of individual social-class effects, the social-class composition of the constituency in which the **voter** lives has declined in importance over time. We found that contextual class effects were consistently significant & fairly constant throughout the period under study. We also find a gradual increase in the amount of constituency variation in vote. Although the proportion of this variation explained by contextual & individual social class has remained fairly constant for Conservative vote, it has decreased for Labour vote. Ultimately, we find evidence of a decline in class voting, but no evidence of a growth in the individualism of voters. 3 Tables, 5 Figures, 1 Appendix, 50 References. Adapted from the source document.

LA: Language English

PY: Publication Year 2002

PT: Publication Type Journal Article (aja)

CP: Country of Publication United Kingdom

DE: Descriptors *Social Class (D781500); *Voting Behavior (D909900); *United Kingdom (D889800); *Class Differences (D135000)

CL: Classification 0925 political sociology/interactions; sociology of political systems, politics, & power

UD: Update 200212

AN: Accession Number 200216413

RE: References 1. Berelson, B., Lazarsfeld, P., & McPhee, W. N. (1954). *Voting: A Study of Opinion Formation in a Presidential Campaign.* University of Chicago Press, Chicago. [Cited by 24] 2. Bodman, A. (1983). *The neighbourhood effect: a test of the Butler-Stokes model.* British Journal of PoliticalScience, 13,243-249. 3. Budge, I. (1999). *Party policy and ideology: reversing the 1950s? In Evans, G.* and Norris, P. (eds) Critical Elections: British Parties and Voters in Long-Term Perspective. Sage, London. [Cited by 5] [and so on]

Reproduced with permission from CSA

Figure 6.1 Example of a bibliographic record

Content and coverage

A database will often include a list of:

- the subject matter covered by the database
- the serials indexed by the database

This information can be of great value for ascertaining whether or not it is worthwhile using the database in question. If it is not available, it may be obtainable from the database provider. For example, the APA[2] (American Psychological Association) that produces the *PsychINFO* database provides a list of the journals indexed, plus other relevant information about the content.

Another aspect of database content that is of interest is the date of coverage. This could have a bearing on other sources the searcher wishes to access if, for example, the coverage timescale does not include all that is required. Some databases do not index articles as far back as others. Some include historical information, but the older the information, the more incomplete it may be. The researcher may find that the database extends further back in time for records with citation details than it does for those with abstracts.

Compare the date ranges of the following databases:

- *Bioengineering Abstracts* from 1993
- *Engineered Materials Abstracts* from 1986
- *Legal Journals Index* (via Westlaw) from 1986
- *Conference Papers Index* from 1982
- *Linguistics and Language Behavior Abstracts* from 1973
- *Econlit* from 1969
- *Inspec* from 1969
- *Sociological Abstracts* 1963 onwards; abstracts from 1974
- *IBSS – International Bibliography of Social Sciences* from 1951
- *PsycINFO* from 1887

The researcher may wish to check frequency of updating, particularly if they are concerned that they are accessing the most up to date information.

Searching options of an online database

Not all databases include all of the following options. Knowing about such issues means the database can be used to its fullest capacity.

Case sensitivity

Most databases are not case sensitive. The legal databases do not require standard punctuation when searching using a legal citation.

Natural language versus structured search queries

Most databases require the use of structured searching, but some accept natural language queries. This facility can be useful if the searcher is unsure of how to formulate a search query, however, it is beneficial for them to learn searching skills (see Chapter 7). A structured search may be aided by the provision of search boxes. A properly constructed query enables the searcher to be highly specific about the information they wish to retrieve.

Quick search versus advanced search

Most databases offer a choice between quick and advanced search. Quick search is useful when an overview is required and the searcher is unconcerned about the numbers of records retrieved. It can also be useful when searching using a narrow term or unusual name (both unlikely to retrieve large numbers of records). The advanced option allows a more precise search, often with comprehensive limiting options.

The search interface

The search interface of a database may offer one or more of the following options:

• A free text box allowing the searcher to type in exactly the search query they require (in a box labelled 'Command-line search', 'terms and connectors' or similar)

- Boxes for the searcher to type in their terms, linked by **Boolean** operators, often in drop-down menus
- Boxes for terms preceded by instructions such as 'including all the terms', 'including some of the terms' or 'including the exact phrase'.

See Chapter 7 for details of searching using Boolean logic and other operators.

Searching in specific fields

Databases are constructed with relevant information assigned to set fields (see Figure 6.1). Searching using specified fields gives a great degree of flexibility and accuracy. This can be achieved by either selecting the field required from a drop-down menu or by including the field abbreviation in the search query. For example, typing the query:

- Greenfield in AU

or

- 'business accounting' in SO

when searching for a particular author or source.

A search within the title field can produce results that are more relevant than searching the entire record or abstract. This is because the item is likely to be about that subject rather than mention it as part of a broader topic and is a good means of narrowing down a search. For example, compare the numbers of results shown in Table 6.1.

It is often possible to select the type of publication in which to run the search (for example, journal articles, conference proceedings or reports). Narrowing down the search in this way helps focus the results.

Searching using the title of a known journal can be useful for:

- finding records of articles to which the searcher knows they have access. The name of the journal can be combined with additional terms to retrieve articles on a chosen topic.

Table 6.1 Comparison of searches in different fields

Field	Numbers of records retrieved
Keyword	12,578
Descriptors	11,688
Abstract	1690
Title	660

Search query 'discourse analysis'

Source: Search run on *Linguistics and Language Behavior Abstracts,*
3 December 2003

- keeping up to date with the contents of a preferred journal

The user may be able to select the journal from a given list or type in the title and search the source field.

Thesaurus search

If a database includes a thesaurus, the searcher is well advised to make use of it. Running a search on a database's own thesaurus can help selection of terms that have been indexed in that database. It also serves to suggest related, broader and narrower terms as well as indicating preferred terms. Terms may have a scope (or explanatory) note giving details of their meaning in the context of the database. The terms in the thesaurus may have live links for easy searching.

Some databases include recognised subject headings as search options. For example, *Medline* includes MeSH subject headings in its controlled vocabulary.

Index search

The index lists the indexed terms in alphabetical order. This can be useful when checking different forms of a word and for browsing. As with thesaurus terms, it may be possible to run a search using a particular term by clicking on a live link.

Related reference search

Some databases (and OPACs) offer an option to retrieve related references, that is, records on the same topic as that which has been retrieved. This is a useful facility, as relevant records can be obtained that may not have been picked up by the search query and might otherwise have been missed. The *Web of Knowledge* database offers this function.

For example, the records retrieved from a search using the query:

multiple sclerosis AND cannabis

includes a reference to:

Killestein J. and Polman C. H. (2003) Cannabis use in multiple sclerosis: Excited interest, *Canadian Journal of Neurological Sciences*, **30** (3): 181–182, August.

Running a search using the 'Find related records' option results in a number of hits including:

Schwenkreis, P. and Tegenthoff, M. (2003) Therapeutic use of cannabinoids in neurology, *Schmerz*, **17** (5): 367–373, October

which was not retrieved in the first search.

Searching across multiple databases

Databases provided by a large supplier such as CSA, who controls a selection of titles, may allow searches of more than one at a time. This option will produce more results, but will save time. A database such as *Medline* or *PsycINFO* comprises a number of smaller databases, divided by date range. In this case the user may select the date ranges most relevant to their search. When dealing with dates, users should be aware of whether the dates are those of the publication of the article, or the date the record was added to the database.

Searching across databases from different providers is becoming more common as the technology and standards are developed to enable this. See Chapter 17.

Understanding records

Numbers of records retrieved

Monitoring the number of records retrieved is key to narrowing down a search to a manageable number of relevant results as the search is honed and relevance is increased. Or conversely, more records are retrieved in a narrow subject area. It can also alert the user to errors in their searching.

Sets

The word 'set' (or 'search number') is used to describe the results of one search query. The database may give the option to combine sets using Boolean operators, or a set may be selected for the query to be edited or added to in some way. The sets may be numbered using the hash symbol. In this case, the user may be able to type a search query using the set number. For example:

#3 AND (monsoon OR rains)

where set 3 was a previous query (such as Bangladesh OR India)

Changing the view

There may be options regarding the detail displayed in a list of results. A list of brief citations is useful when scanning results for relevance or quickly identifying records of possible interest. In order to evaluate the content of an article more accurately for relevance, the searcher will wish to access other fields such as the abstract and descriptors if they are available. They may be able to select the fields they wish to see displayed. Options that might be available are:

- citation: brief details of author, title, publication, volume, issue and date

- citation and abstract: the above plus the abstract
- full record: all the information included in the record
- full record omit references: if a database includes references in the record, they can make the record lengthy
- KWIC: Key Word In Context. Short extracts from the record that include the keyword; useful when evaluating the relevance of a record. If a device such as truncation has been used, the searcher can easily identify any unexpected rogue words, or homographs, only one of which is relevant. The searcher can then edit the search to make the results more relevant.

Whatever the display selected, it is common to find the search terms displayed in bold or coloured type.

Records are usually displayed in reverse chronological order of date of publication (most recent first), but the user can often choose the way in which results are presented.

Navigating around the results

The searcher is usually able to navigate around the results by either scrolling using an arrow symbol (◀ ▶), by specifying the number of the result they wish to display or by clicking on a 'next record' or 'previous record' button. Having displayed an individual record, there will be a button or link to return to the list of results.

There may be an option to search within the results, enabling the search to be narrowed down.

Links within the record

Terms within a record might be hyperlinked: clicking on them enables discovery of other records that include those terms. It is common to find these links for the:

- author's name
- title of journal
- descriptors

Some of these options will result in large numbers of results, but it is a useful means of finding other records with similar characteristics, or articles by the same author.

Managing results

Marking records

Most databases allow users to mark (or tag) records using a check box or 'mark records' button. This means that the researcher can mark those records they have identified as being of most relevance, then click on the 'show marked records' button to strip out those not selected, leaving a shorter, apposite list.

Printing, saving or e-mailing records

In order to manage research well, searchers should be diligent in keeping records of relevant references by saving them in some way. A printed list is useful when visiting a library to track down sources. It is advisable to retain an electronic copy of references so that the text can be easily edited when creating a list of references or bibliography, saving time retyping the details. The electronic copy can be made either by downloading or by sending an e-mail to oneself. Some databases also include a fax option in addition to the above.

If using bibliographic software (see Chapter 14), results can sometimes be downloaded directly to the chosen package. If available, each database should be checked for the means of doing this.

There may be the option to select the sections of the record(s) for printing, saving or e-mailing, for example saving entire records, or just citations and abstracts. It is often possible to select exactly which record(s) should be saved, for example, current record displayed, marked records, all records or specific selected records.

Search history

Searches run in one session form a search history. This will be shown either on the search page where the search history can be seen building up with each subsequent search, or on a separate page. Using this facility, searches already performed in a session can be combined, edited or re-run.

The search history can be saved or printed which is valuable for record-keeping purposes.

Saving searches

If searches in a session are saved, they can be revisited during a later session on that database. The results can be accessed or the search re-run to update it.

Alerts

Alerts are a means of keeping up to date (see Chapter 16).

Quirks

Because databases vary, the user should take care to notice any quirks associated with the one they are using. Their librarian will be able to help in this respect and will alert users to possible anomalies.

For example, *Science Direct* requires that the search history facility is turned on before embarking on a search. Likewise, when using *Web of Knowledge*, users have to click 'submit marked records' on each separate page, otherwise the marks are lost.

Logging off from a database using its own logging off button (when available) can be important, particularly if the licensing agreement is for a limited number of concurrent users. In such a case, not logging off can result in another user being unable to access the database for some time.

Help function

The 'Help' functions of databases vary from those which are comprehensive with an inbuilt search facility or index, to those which are of little use. However, the researcher should check the help available as it will engender more efficient use of the database and its functions.

Catalogues and bibliographies

The RSLG (Research Support Libraries Group) report of a review of higher education libraries states that 'the OPAC is the most popular discovery tool for researchers overall' (RSLG 2003, paragraph 64). Catalogues, either libraries' or publishers', are a means of discovering items. Searching the home library catalogue is advantageous because access to items will be easy. For broader coverage or when searching for highly specialist items, use of union catalogues such as COPAC or the British Library will be necessary.

Book publishers should have the most up to date information regarding their own products but the drawback is being forced to check many separate catalogues. They do not include information on out of print titles. Publishers' catalogues are often available both in print and online.

Some publishers focus on particular subject areas and researchers become familiar with the names associated with their own subject. For example, the publisher Multilingual Matters specializes in titles associated with languages and linguistics and Thomas Telford Books provides texts about civil engineering and construction.

Most major disciplines have a bibliography that covers the subject. If printed, they will not necessarily be particularly current, but can be of great use for discovering previously published works. The *BNB* (*British National Bibliography*) covers all disciplines, including forthcoming titles and is regularly updated: monthly on CD-ROM and weekly in print.

Online bookshops can be used as online catalogues for the discovery of resources.

Research libraries

For the purposes of this chapter, the term, 'research library' can be defined as a large library with an extensive collection of national interest that supports researchers in one or more disciplines and which might act as an archive.

UK national libraries

National libraries maintain collections of all national printed publications issued in their own country. This is achieved by a system of legal deposit where either the publishers are obliged to provide the library with a copy of every item they publish, or the library is entitled to request a copy of every item published (see Chapter 2). All provide online catalogues which can be freely searched. The national library might also issue a national bibliography of printed publications, such as the *BNB* in the UK.

Other specialist national libraries in the UK include:

- The National Art Library at the Victoria and Albert Museum[3]
- The National Library for the Blind[4]
- The National Electronic Library for Health[5] (NHS – National Health Service)
- The National Electronic Library for Mental Health[6] (NHS)
- BFI (British Film Institute) National Library[7]
- Manx National Heritage, National Library and Archive[8]

Non-UK national libraries

The Library of Congress in the US retains vast holdings and provides online catalogues for searching its extensive collections. The catalogue allows expert search techniques for better retrieval.

The *Gabriel* Web site is described as 'the gateway to Europe's national libraries' (Gabriel 2004) with information about the National libraries of Europe, their online services and exhibitions.

The European Library (TEL), an initiative funded by the European Commission, is due to be launched at the end of 2004 (Woldering 2003). It is an online interface that will enable access to the collections of the European national libraries. Consultation with publishers is ongoing to resolve issues associated with the incorporation of electronic materials such as legal deposit, copyright and suitable business models. In the first instance, as well as details of non-digital items, only freely available electronic resources and those digitized by the libraries themselves will be available. Multilingual and translation facilities are being investigated. TEL will provide a pan-European resource for researchers who will be able to search for collections as individual items. The *Gabriel* service (see above) will be incorporated into TEL.

Other countries' national libraries online catalogues are freely available on the WWW. Links to many catalogues may be found via the British Library's Web site or on one of the Library of Congress Internet resource pages. The British Library is one of the partners in the MACS Project (Multilingual ACcess to Subjects) sponsored by the Conference of European National Librarians (CENL). The other partners are:

- Swiss National Library (SNL)
- Bibliothèque nationale de France (BnF)
- Die Deutsche Bibliothek (DDB)

The project is developing a means of achieving multilingual, multi-site searching across national libraries in Europe. Users will be able to search the catalogues of the project's partner libraries simultaneously in the language of their choice (English, French, German).

University research libraries

Although all university libraries tailor their collections to support the research within their own institutions, some retain extensive collections that will be of interest to researchers on a national level. Of the six legal deposit libraries in the UK and Ireland, three are university libraries:

- Bodleian Library, Oxford
- University Library, Cambridge
- Trinity College, Dublin

These collections are searchable via OPACs.

The John Rylands University Library of Manchester (JRULM) is the largest academic library in the UK which is not a legal deposit library. It has broad subject coverage and some special collections.

Other university libraries hold extensive and specialist collections in selected subject areas. For example:

- the social sciences collection at the British Library of Political and Economic Science
- the legal collection at the IALS[9]

Specialist research libraries

Researchers in specialist subject areas are often able to locate resources in specialist libraries. These may be the libraries of professional bodies, charitable organizations or centres of research excellence that are not educational institutions, for example museums. The *ASLIB Directory of Information Sources in the United Kingdom* (Reynard 2002) includes entries for many of these libraries (see above).

Some specialist libraries in main subject areas, all of which have OPACs, are as follows:

Engineering and Mathematics:

- Institution of Electrical Engineers[10]
- RIBA (Royal Institute of British Architects) British Architectural Library[11]
- London Mathematical Society[12]

Health and Life Sciences:

- The Wellcome Library for the History and Understanding of Medicine
- Natural History Museum Library[13]
- Royal Horticultural Society[14]
- National Oceanographic Library, Southampton[15]
- Centre for Ecology and Hydrology[16]

Humanities and Art:

- British Library Digital Catalogue of Illuminated Manuscripts (DigCIM)
- The Courtauld Institute of Art[17]
- The London Library collection of books in all European languages in the humanities

Physical Sciences:

- The Royal Society of Chemistry[18]
- The Royal Society[19]

Social Sciences, Business and Law:

- The Women's library[20]
- London Business School[21]

Research Libraries Group (RLG)

The Research Libraries Group comprises around 160 institutions including universities, national libraries, archives, museums, independent research collections, historical societies and others. All retain and manage extensive research collections. Members are mainly in the US, but there are others all over the world. The group provides a union catalogue for subscribers (which is being further developed under the *RedLightGreen* project), but there is free access to the Web pages of member institutions.

What's in London's Libraries (WiLL)

The London Libraries Development Agency is working to develop a means of cross-searching public library catalogues and community information databases in 33 London boroughs from any networked terminal in London public libraries (a project funded by the *People's Network Excellence Fund*). The resulting system, named WiLL[22], includes some museum and archive databases.

Public libraries

Public library collections are usually of limited use to those undertaking large-scale research projects. However, they can be valuable in areas such as local history. Many have OPACs covering the county or area libraries.

Open access journals

Open access journal suppliers have search facilities on their Web sites that will allow users to discover relevant articles: some have well-designed advanced search options. These services are growing and of increasing importance to the researcher (see Chapter 11).

Other sources and types of information

Databases that contain records of other formats, such as audio visual materials, can be searched in similar ways to bibliographic databases. For example, the AHDS (Arts and Humanities Data Service)[23] provides access to databases in the fields of archaeology, language and linguistics, history, performing arts and the visual arts, the British Universities Film and Video Council (BUFVC)[24] provides access to the *Moving Image Gateway* (MIG) and the *British Universities Newsreel Database* (BUND), and the *Education Image Gallery*[25] (EIG) holds around 50,000 images for use in education. The COPAC union catalogue has a map search option which limits the search to items such as maps, nautical charts, atlases and topographical drawings.

For grey literature, there is the SIGLE database (see Chapter 4). *Zetoc*, the database created jointly by the British Library and the JISC, contains bibliographic details of many thousands of conference proceedings and journals' tables of contents from all disciplines. It is available to UK further and higher education institutions.

New York Public Library catalogue[26] can be of great use for checking bibliographic details of US titles (in addition to the

Library of Congress catalogue). It also includes audio visual materials, maps and artefacts as well as access to the Dance Collection catalogue and the Schomburg Center for Research in Black Culture catalogue.

The BOPCRIS[27] (British Official Publications Collaborative Reader Information Service) catalogue can be used to discover British Official publications published between 1688 and 1995. Abstracts are provided for many records. The Public Record Office provides PROCAT[28], its online catalogue, and other catalogues that have details of its and other collections of holdings. The TSO Official Documents Web site[29] contains details of items from January 2001 and an archive 1994–2001.

References and citation searching

Scrutinizing the references included in works and performing a citation search (see Chapter 8) are valuable methods of discovering information.

Selecting sources relevant to the subject

Searchers often develop tunnel vision when it comes to using databases. They know and use one database which covers their chosen subject, and ignore others. It is true that there is usually a large, reliable and well-known database for most broad subject areas, but that does not mean it is the only resource. Nor does it mean that other more general databases do not cover the subject. For example, subscribers can access the *British Library Inside* database to search for research journals and individual papers from conferences in all subject disciplines. Researchers should familiarize themselves with the range of databases available to them, including general titles. For example, *Science Direct* from the publisher Elsevier does not imply from its title that it will be of any use to researchers in subjects other than pure science. In fact, the subject coverage includes journal titles in the fields of:

- arts and humanities

- business, management and accounting
- economics, econometrics and finance

Checking the content and coverage of databases (see above) is imperative for running a comprehensive search or finding an item not listed in the chosen favoured database.

Key points

- Information discovery is the process of finding details of relevant information
- Researchers need to find the details, bibliographic or otherwise, of items that are required
- Online bibliographic databases are a means of finding bibliographic details of items
- Searchers should check the facilities and help function of each database
- Records that have been discovered and searches and search histories can be saved for future reference
- Catalogues, bibliographies and lists of references can be used to discover items
- Researchers should use a variety of databases for comprehensive searching and beware database tunnel vision

---

7

THE ONLINE SEARCHING PROCESS

The importance of planning a search

Someone running a search on a database or search engine might sit at the computer, access a favourite database/search engine, type in a word and see what happens, with little or no prior thought given to the method of searching. The consequence of this unplanned searching is that the searcher may stumble across some relevant references fairly quickly – or not. There may be innumerable hits, or very few, and what is retrieved may be irrelevant. Faced with this unsatisfactory result, the searcher will then enter an alternative search term which may produce similarly unsuccessful results to the first. This process may be repeated until either the searcher has gathered what they think is a reasonable list of records for the task in hand, or until they become so frustrated that they give up.

Any suitable references resulting from this type of search are a result of luck rather than planning and, most importantly, the searcher may have missed key references. A familiar scenario is one where a piece of work is presented with large numbers of references, most of which are peripheral to the subject and omitting work by well-known specialists in the field of study.

It is important that those undertaking any type of research are able to find the information they need efficiently. In the first instance of planning the research project, it is vital that researchers are fully aware of the work of others so that time is not wasted and work is not repeated unwittingly. Expert searching skills will aid this process. When undertaking research for papers or books that are to be published or sent for peer review, it is important that references to relevant publications are not omitted and that the author demonstrates a complete knowledge of the current situation in their chosen field.

Sadly the poor searching scenario such as the one above happens all too frequently. Kate Hodgson of CMS Cameron McKenna wrote of the searching techniques of legal trainees:

> Most trainees use such poor search strategies and techniques on both the web and commercial databases. Over 80% of searches carried out are for one single word. The concepts searched for are not thought-out, the key terms are not identified, relationships between key terms are not thought through, and Boolean logic might as well be a clue in a Vulcan crossword.
>
> (Hodgson 2002: 14)

Poor search techniques are not only used by legal trainees. The JUSTEIS (JISC Usage Surveys: Trends in Electronic Information Services) project investigated the behaviour of end users of electronic information services. One finding was that 'postgraduates may be focused and persistent in their searching [of search engines] but do not necessarily employ cohesive strategies' (Armstrong et al. 2000: section 6.3.3). The user behaviour section concludes that 'given the wide range of engines used and the haphazard nature of much of the searching, some thought might be given to ways of encouraging students to use the Internet more effectively.' These findings are applicable to search techniques using structured databases.

Single word searching *can* be useful when using specific specialist terms or as part of a more complex search strategy where terms will be combined later, but searchers should not rely solely on this technique. In cases where the single search term is broad (for example, 'sociology' or 'perception'), the numbers of hits may be extremely high and therefore unmanageable.

Having explained the problems associated with poor search techniques resulting from a lack of initial planning, the benefits of planning a search strategy should be noted.

Planning a search strategy:

• results in the retrieval of relevant references
• avoids omitting key references
• is more likely to retrieve a manageable number of results
• uses time efficiently

The aim of planning a search is to retrieve a *manageable* number of *relevant* results.

Searching using successful techniques can be time-consuming. It is, however, far preferable to spend the time profitably, retrieving relevant results rather than wasting precious time gathering poor results.

The online searching process

The searching process is both iterative and heuristic. It is a circular rather than a linear process. It can best be defined as being complete when the searcher retrieves records that they have already identified as of use and no new relevant records are thrown up. In some ways, the search can never be described as complete owing to the fact that additional terms and new information will be encountered as the research progresses.

The search process comprises the following steps:

- PLAN: IDENTIFY the terms and FORMULATE the search strategy
- RUN the search
- RETRIEVE a manageable number of relevant results
- EVALUATE the results
- SAVE the results
- MODIFY and re-run the search

(see Figure 7.1) all the time keeping records of the process.

What follows is a description of the process when searching online, but many of the techniques are also relevant when searching using print sources.

How to plan a search strategy

Tempting though it is to begin using large and powerful databases straight away, the following method is recommended prior to the search.

The practical method of planning a search strategy depends on the preferences of the individual. Some will opt for paper and pencil, others may use a word processor and some will draw spider diagrams or Mind Maps® (see Tony Buzan's books on the subject, including *How to Mind Map* (Buzan 2002), perhaps with the aid of specialist software.

The researcher should plan the next five steps before proceeding with the search.

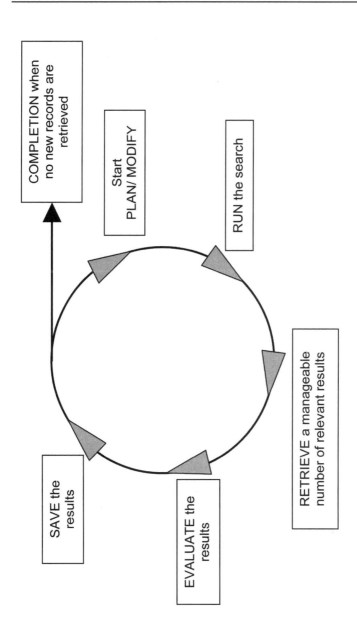

Figure 7.1 The online search process

1. Identifying search terms
2. Limiting the search
3. Truncation, wildcards and phrases
4. Combining terms 1 (Boolean logic)
5. Combining terms 2 (using other connectors)

See Figure 7.2 for a diagrammatic representation of these steps.

Step 1: Identifying search terms

The area of research and the information need will already have been defined (see Chapters 1 and 5). Using the results of this, the next step is to focus on the words that will be used to find information. The terms which are selected for searching are the foundation from which the research grows.

When reading around the subject in the initial stages of the work, keep a record of significant words which may later be used for searching. Together with the formal designation of concepts and search terms, these words can be used to build up a matrix of keywords for the execution of the search.

It is beneficial to have a dictionary, a thesaurus and, possibly, encyclopaedias to hand, including any specialist subject publications such as a dictionary of the subject area (for example, a dictionary of economics). Research supervisors and other specialists can offer help with the selection of search terms.

The main topics can be broken down into sub-topics and linked areas which will also suggest possible search terms. To achieve this the researcher might i) create a list using main and subheadings, ii) compile a table or iii) draw a Mind Map® or diagram. For example, the hypothesis might be:
'The news media in the UK is more concerned with sensationalism than balanced reporting'.

Figures 7.3, 7.4 and 7.5 show representations of topics as headings and subheadings, a table and a diagram respectively. They are by no means exhaustive, but give an outline of a possible solution.

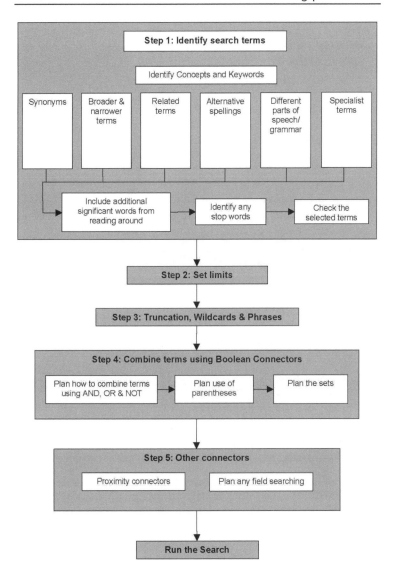

Figure 7.2 The five search steps

'The news media in the UK is more concerned with sensationalism than balanced reporting'

1 News Media

1.1 Individual characteristics of selected publications

Reporting styles

Use of language

Use of images and other audio visual devices

Readership/Viewing or listening profiles

The coverage of different subject areas (for example, politics, human interest, environment)

1.2 Types of news media in the UK

Newspapers (broadsheet & tabloid)

Television (Public service & commercial; land, cable and satellite)

Radio (Public service & commercial)

Internet news

1.3 The people involved

Reporters

Editors

Newspaper owners

Readers

Subjects of the stories and so on

2 Sensationalism

2.1 Define sensationalism

Dictionary definition

Definition used in these investigations

2.2 Attitudes towards sensationalism in the UK

Attitudes of the general populace

2.3 The Law in the UK

Privacy laws

Libel and slander

3 Balanced reporting

3.1 Define balanced reporting

Dictionary definition

Definition used in these investigations

3.2 Commercial interests

Vested interests

Viewing/listening/readership figures

3.3 Impartiality

Figure 7.3 Topics shown as main headings and subheadings

Main Title
'The news media in the UK is more concerned with sensationalism than balanced reporting'

Concept 1 News media			Concept 2 Sensationalism			Concept 3 Balanced reporting		
Topic area 1 Individual characteristics of selected publications	**Topic area 2** Types of news media in the UK	**Topic area 3** The people involved	**Topic area 1** Define sensationalism	**Topic area 2** Attitudes towards sensationalism in the UK	**Topic area 3** The Law in the UK	**Topic area 1** Define balanced reporting	**Topic area 2** Commercial interests	**Topic area 3** Impartiality
Reporting styles	Newspapers (broadsheet & tabloid)	Reporters	Dictionary definition	Attitudes of the general populace	Privacy laws Libel and slander	Dictionary definition	Vested interests	
Use of language	Television (Public service & commercial; land, cable and satellite)	Editors	Definition used in these investigations			Definition used in these investigations	Viewing/listening/readership figures	
Use of images and other audio visual devices	Radio (Public service & commercial) Internet news	Newspaper owners						
Readership/Viewing or listening profiles		Readers						
The coverage of different subject areas (for example, politics, human interest, environment)		Subjects of the stories and so on						

Figure 7.4 Topics shown in table format

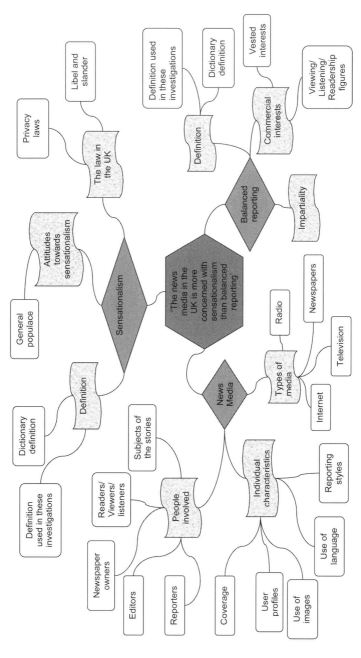

Figure 7.5 Topics shown as a diagram

Concepts

Using the title (or statement or question) as a starting point, extract the main concepts (topics or ideas) and list them in a table or use them as a starting point for a diagram.

It is advisable to limit the number of concepts to a maximum of four. Any more, and the search becomes over-complex. A large number of concepts may indicate that the area of research has not been succinctly defined or is too broad.

Example title:

• With reference to organizations in the UK, to what extent has the 'glass ceiling' been shattered?

Figure 7.6 shows an example of the concepts using a table. The topics from above can be included in the plans.

Synonyms

The researcher's title or hypothesis may use one particular word, but other articles written on the same topic may include a similar one instead. The effect of not including synonyms in the search is that the records retrieved will exclude relevant material that doesn't happen to use identical words. The concept term 'organization' in the example above has a number of synonyms, including:

• company
• corporation
• federation
• firm
• institution

Use of a thesaurus will make the task of identifying synonyms easier. Structured databases often include a thesaurus which the researcher should consider using.

Include both the abbreviation and the full words in the search strategy. For example:

With reference to organizations in the UK, to what extent has the 'glass ceiling' been shattered?			
CONCEPTS	Glass ceiling	Organizations	UK
SYNONYMS			
BROADER TERMS			
NARROWER TERMS			
RELATED TERMS			
ALTERNATIVE SPELLINGS			
PARTS OF SPEECH			

Figure 7.6 Example of concepts shown as a table

- UK   United Kingdom
- EOC   Equal Opportunities Commission
- kHz   kilohertz

Figures present a similar case. Include amounts in both figures and words when dealing with situations such as dates:

- 1930s   nineteen thirties
- 14th century   fourteenth century

Hyphens can present a problem, so err on the side of caution and include both forms, with and without the hyphen if appropriate. For example:

Neoclassical   neo-classical

Always check the help function of the database for guidance.

An area of which to be aware is where a change of name has taken place, for example:

• Department for Education
• Department of Education and Science (DES)
• Department for Education and Skills (DfES)

Go through each search term carefully, identifying the relevant synonyms and include them in the table or diagram. Table 7.1 demonstrates how many records might be missed if synonyms are not used.

Table 7.1 Search using synonyms for the term 'organizations'

Term/Synonym	Numbers of records retrieved
Organizations	778
Firms	888
Companies	471
Institutions	1357
Corporations	206

Source: Searches run on *IBSS* (easy search: title field), 19 January 2004

When checking the databases' thesauri, the searcher may encounter the instruction 'Use for . . .' This occurs when the indexer has selected a particular term instead of one or more other possibilities. For example, one might encounter:

• Workers: *Use for* employee/employees

In this case, the query should not include the term employees, but substitute the term workers.

Broader and narrower terms

For each concept, broader and narrower terms should be considered as possibilities for inclusion in the search. One can think of broader and narrower terms using the analogy of a man. Progressively broader terms could be:

- Human being
- Mammal
- Vertebrate

and so on.

Progressively narrower terms could be:

- Blood circulatory system
- Blood
- Red blood cells

and so on.

It can be helpful to think of viewing terms through both a telescope for a broader view and a microscope for the detail. The result is a hierarchy of terms. One can think of keywords as part of a hierarchy with broader terms above and more specific, narrower terms below (see Figure 7.7).

In the 'glass ceiling' example, broader terms for UK might be Europe or the British Isles. A narrower term for UK might be the individual countries: England, Scotland, Northern Ireland and Wales, or particular regions or counties (such as North West England or Lancashire). The researcher should use their judgement to decide which terms are relevant to their search and therefore included.

Databases sometimes use an 'Explode' function to list narrower terms. This can be a helpful method of drilling down to the most relevant search terms, ignoring irrelevant terms.

The use of broader and narrower terms depends on the individual piece of work. For example, a researcher may decide that it is necessary to include narrower terms in the search strategy, but not broader terms. In the example, the researcher would not

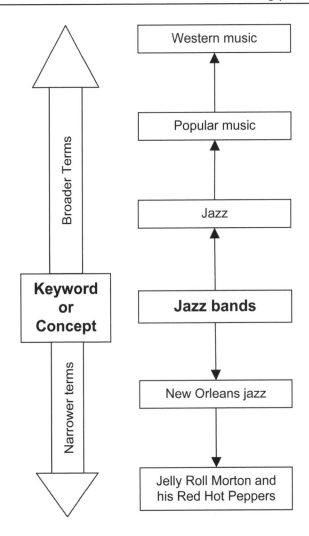

Figure 7.7 Broader and narrower terms

wish to include Europe and might limit any retrieved records to items concerned solely with the UK. They should be aware though, of the types of results that this action will exclude (see Boolean NOT searching below). The reasons for inclusion/ exclusion of broader and/or narrower terms may include:

- the numbers of retrieved records are too many/too few
- the concept is such a specialist or specific term as to be the most narrow available
- a broader term would be so broad as to be irrelevant
- the searcher would like an overview of the general situation in order to place the chosen topic in context
- examples in specific areas are required
- an example of an identical test situation is required therefore broader or narrower terms are irrelevant

Related terms

A related term is one which is linked to the search terms by subject matter, but which may not be included in the synonyms or broader or narrower terms. In the example, terms related to 'glass ceiling' might be:

- promotion
- personnel management
- discrimination
- women

Subject knowledge and experience should be used to select related terms to be included in the search. Some databases include a function to retrieve records that have been indexed as related records to those already retrieved (see Chapter 6). See also the section on evaluation of the results below. If a database includes a thesaurus, related terms may be included.

Alternative spellings

Many words have alternative spellings, especially US spellings, and it is important to be aware of them. If the search is run using a single spelling option, the database may not automatically retrieve records with alternative(s), leaving the results incomplete and the searcher unaware that they have missed potentially large numbers of records. Table 7.2 demonstrates this point.

Common variants in spelling are shown in Table 7.3.

Table 7.2 Example of searches using alternative spellings

	Search term	Numbers of records retrieved
Search 1	behaviour	34,041
Search 2	behavior	416,455
Difference between searches 1 & 2		382,414

Source: Search run on the APA PsychINFO database without limits selected, 19 January 2004

Table 7.3 Common variants in spelling

	Common spelling variants	Example
UK and US English	our/or	Humour/humor
	s/z	organisation/ organization
	double letters	woollen/woolen
	re/er	centre/center
	difference in word	speciality/specialty
Archaic words		matins/mattins
Words with Latin/ Greek root	Ligatures	encyclopædia/fœtus encyclopaedia/foetus encyclopedia/fetus
New accepted simplified spelling		sulphur/sulfur
Foreign words	ö/oe	Schröder/Schroeder poppadom/ poppadam
Colloquialisms/Slang		pukka/pukkah/pucca

Databases vary in their ability to recognize and incorporate alternative spellings. It is safer to assume that it will not automatically incorporate any alternatives. Find out about the individual database's capability by checking the 'help' function of the database, or briefly scan the results to see whether or not they are included.

At this point in the planning process, check the broader, narrower and related terms selected for synonyms and alternative spellings.

Different parts of speech/grammar

Not only should plurals of nouns be included where appropriate, but also different parts of speech.

Some databases will include plurals automatically when running a search. Others will include common plurals such as the addition of a letter 's' or 'es', but check whether or not more complex plurals are automatically included. These may include words such as:

* party/parties
* thesaurus/thesauri
* criterion/criteria

There are cases when one should consider all forms of the words in addition to the plural. This can include noun, verb, adjective, past tense and so on. In the example above the searcher may choose to use some or all of the following:

* organization
* organizational
* organizationally

not forgetting to include the alternative s/z spelling. In this case 'organize' and 'organized' can probably be ignored.

Phrase or separate words

When referring to searching queries, a phrase can be defined as two or more words that are required consecutively and in a given order, for example 'League of Nations' or 'chicken pox'. When a phrase occurs amongst the search terms, the searcher must decide whether or not they want to search for those words as a phrase, or split the words and search for them either individually or in a different word order. This will create quite different searches.

One would probably choose not to split the phrase in the example above. 'Glass ceiling' has a specific meaning and the words are unlikely to be used in a different form (although there is the possibility that the record may contain the same words used differently, but with the same meaning for example, 'ceiling of glass'). 'European Court of Human Rights' is another example of a phrase with a specific meaning that should remain intact when searching. Whereas a searcher faced with the phrase 'juvenile crime' is likely to consider using the words 'juvenile' and 'crime' separately.

Specialist terms

Use of specialist terms will often narrow a search down and produce particularly relevant records if the term appears in the title, abstract or indexing terms. This can create difficulties if the term is relatively new and few records include it. Alternatively, use of a specialist term can help reduce the numbers of results when too many are being retrieved. There is often no alternative for a specialist term, for example, 'Stroop test' is a particular type of test familiar to psychologists for which there is no obvious alternative.

Checking the terms selected

Having worked through the steps above to arrive at a selection of search terms, the searcher should check the completed table or diagram carefully for omissions. Figure 7.8 is by no means exhaustive, but should give an impression of how the finished table may appear.

Noise or stop words

Databases are usually designed not to accept searches that include common words such as 'by', 'but', 'if', and so on. Other

With reference to organizations in the UK, to what extent has the 'glass ceiling' been shattered?			
CONCEPTS	**Glass ceiling**	**Organizations**	**UK**
SYNONYMS		firms	United Kingdom
		companies	
		institutions	
		corporations	
		enterprises	
BROADER TERMS			Western Europe
			Europe
NARROWER TERMS		SMEs	Great Britain
		small and medium enterprises	Britain
		plc	Northern Ireland
		public limited company	Scotland
			Wales
			England
RELATED TERMS	promotion	businesses	
	personnel management	workplace	
	discrimination	offices	
	equal opportunities	management structure	
	Equal Opportunites Commission		
	women		
	female		
ALTERNATIVE SPELLINGS	EOC	organizations	
PARTS OF SPEECH	promoted	organization	British
	discriminatory	institutional	Scottish
	discriminate	corporate	
	woman	corporation	
	females		
	sex discrimination		
	gender discrimination		

Figure 7.8 Completed table of search terms

words that may not be accepted are those that can be used as a command, for example 'within' or 'near' (see below). These disallowed words are called stop (or noise) words. The database may display a message informing the user that a disallowed word has been included or that too many records will be retrieved. Check whether stop words may be included perhaps by the addition of quotation marks: they are usually allowed if they form part of a phrase, for example

- 'near miss'
- 'trial by jury'

Step 2: Limiting the search

In addition to defining what is required from the search, it is equally important to define what is not required and how the search may be limited. The scope of the search will already have been decided (see Chapter 5).

Databases vary in the limiting options they offer and each should be checked to see what is available. Take advantage of the limiting options as they will enable the search to be more specific and the results more relevant.

Common limiting options include:

- language: there is little point in retrieving results in a language that is incomprehensible to the researcher (unless translating facilities are available) and many databases index items in foreign languages. Check the language of the document, as the database record may be in, say, English, but the full text of the item in a different language.
- date of publication: researchers may wish to retrieve records from a particular period for example, only the most recent publications.
- type of publication: in addition to references to journal articles, many databases contain references to items such as book reviews, dissertation abstracts, audio cassettes, reports and books.

Databases vary in the limit options they offer: some can be sparse whilst others contain many options. For example, the *Compendex* database quick search offers limiting options of:

- document type
- treatment type (that is, the viewpoint of the document)
- language
- date of publication

PsycINFO has a comprehensive selection of limits including:

- language
- publication type
- publication year
- URL
- age group
- audience type
- document type
- population

Step 3: Truncation, wildcards and phrases

Truncation

Truncation is sometimes referred to as stemming or root expansion. The words which are identified as search terms when considering different parts of speech often have the beginning of the word (or stem) in common. For example,

- organization
- organizations
- organizational

all have the same *organizatio* ... as the start of the word.

A specified symbol can take the place of the remainder of the word. This enables a search for a number of words using a single query, therefore saving time and the search becoming unmanageably complex.

The truncated search term may be:

- organizatio*
- organizatio?
- organizatio$

or other variation.

The symbols used for truncation vary, so check which symbol to use for each database. Using the incorrect symbol will result in unreliable results or no results.

Before searching using a truncated term, check it will not result in unintended references. For example:

- philan*

will not only retrieve philanthrope, philanthropic, philanthropine, philanthropism, philanthropist but also philanderer! Use a dictionary to help select and check truncation possibilities.

Problems may arise when searching using truncation on short words, for example when searching for the singular and plural of the word pit:

- pit? In this case use of the truncation symbol will retrieve many unwanted terms including pitch; pitted; pithy; pitchfork; pituitary. If the searcher only requires the plural form of this word, it would be better to use an OR search (see below) or a single wildcard symbol (if it can take the place of no character as well as one character).
- pit OR pits
- pit*

Note that use of the wildcard will also retrieve 'pith'.

Wildcards

A wildcard (or universal character) is a symbol that can be used in place of one character, no character or sometimes a group of characters. They may be incorporated within or at the end of a word. Wildcards are not usually permitted at the start of words.

Like truncation symbols, databases vary and the 'Help' function should be checked to find which symbol should be used, and how it should be incorporated. In the following examples, the symbol? has been used as the wildcard.

Single character wildcards can be used to replace one character at a time only. For example, when searching for words such as woman and women:

- wom?n

More than one wildcard may be used, each representing one character, for example:

- bacterioly???

will retrieve bacteriolysis and bacteriolytic

Depending on the database, the wildcard may also represent no character, useful when searching for alternative spellings. For example:

- behavio?r

will retrieve both the UK and US versions of this word. It may also be used at the end of a word, for example for retrieving singular and plurals:

- trustee?

Some databases allow the use of multi-character wildcards. These can take the place of a group of characters and can be used for alternative spellings, for example:

- encyclop?dia

will retrieve all spellings of the word.

Phrases

Phrases can make the retrieved results more relevant as there are more criteria for the search. When using a phrase with which to search, some databases require double inverted commas, for example:

- "glass ceiling"

The searcher should be aware of the default of the database they are using. For some, two or more words as the search query will automatically result in a phrase search (for example, *Web of Knowledge*), others default to an AND or an OR search, which will produce quite different results (see below).

Step 4: Combining terms 1 (Boolean logic)

Being able to combine search terms in a meaningful way allows the searcher to be specific about what they wish to retrieve from the database. When executed properly, this means that the results should contain relevant records and ignore others.

Boolean logic is named after the English mathematician George Boole (d. 1864) who developed a method of notation for logic statements. There are three Boolean connectors (or operators) that can be used between the search terms:

- AND
- OR
- NOT

As with truncation and wildcards, each database should be checked for the actual operators as they vary (for example, some use AND NOT or BUT NOT instead of NOT). Use of these connectors can be most clearly represented using Venn diagrams. Each circle represents the records containing the given term.

AND

Combining two (or more) terms with the AND connector means that the results must contain both (or all) of the words. This means records that include fewer than all of the terms will be ignored.

Using an AND search will narrow down the number of results. Figure 7.9 demonstrates the search query: university AND funding. The area where the circles overlap represents the records that will be retrieved. The remainder will be ignored.

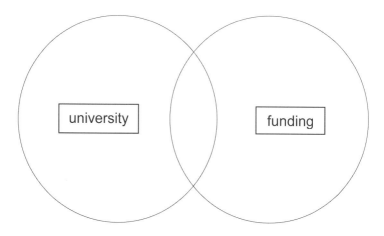

Figure 7.9 Search query: university AND funding

Adding more terms using AND narrows the results further. Figure 7.10 shows the effect of adding another term (UK) to the previous query: the area where the three circles overlap in the centre representing the records retrieved has shrunk in size from that in Figure 7.9.

Some databases will allow the use of a symbol such as & or + instead of typing AND.

OR

The OR connector is generally used when there are two or more alternative terms and the searcher requires that records containing both (or all) are included in the search. Consequently, an OR connector broadens the search. Figure 7.11 shows a basic OR search.

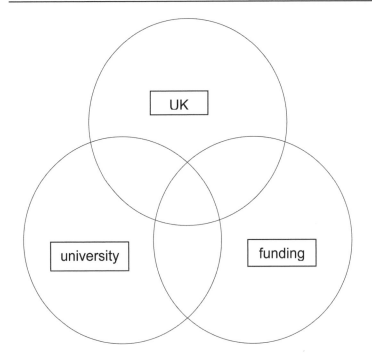

Figure 7.10 Search query: university AND funding AND UK

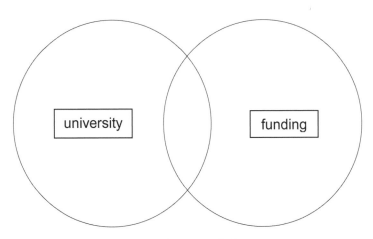

Figure 7.11 Search query: infants OR babies

NOT

The NOT connector is used when a particular term is to be excluded from the search. This may be either to limit the search or to clarify meaning. For example, for articles about continental Europe only, and not including the UK

- Europe NOT UK

An example of clarifying meaning could be:

- macintosh NOT computer

and other homographs

- ash NOT tree

Figure 7.12 shows the effect of the search query Europe NOT UK. In this example, records including the word 'Europe' will be retrieved, but if there is a single instance of the word 'UK' it will be ignored. This is a useful means of disregarding irrelevant records, but the area of overlap where both terms appear will not be retrieved.

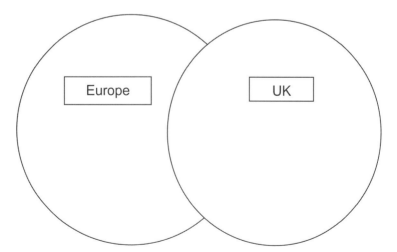

Figure 7.12 Search query: Europe NOT UK

The searcher should use their skill and judgement when dealing with homographs as to which word(s) to exclude. Evaluation of the results will aid the decision (see below).

Some databases will allow the use of a symbol such as % instead of typing NOT.

Implied Boolean logic

Another search option that the searcher may encounter is that of Boolean logic that has been disguised to make the search page more user-friendly.

Find results:

- with all the words: equates to an AND search
- with some of the terms/with at least one of the words: equates to an OR search
- without the terms/that excludes these words: equates to a NOT search
- with the exact phrase: is a phrase search

Additionally, search within the results performs an AND search.

Parentheses

When combining terms it is easy unintentionally to create a search strategy that is ambiguous. In order to avoid this many databases allow the use of parentheses.

The 'Help' function may give the order in which the search commands are prioritized. Parentheses are usually considered first. Check this information on the database(s) being used.

The need for parentheses can be demonstrated by a simple mathematical problem:

a) 6 (4 + 5)
b) 6 × 4 + 5
c) 6 × 4 + 6 × 5

The answer to a) is 54. To calculate this correctly the solver *must* first solve the parentheses either by solving the sum in parentheses or multiplying each number in the parentheses by 6. The answer to b) could be 29 (that is 24 + 5) or 54 (that is 6 × 9) depending on the order which the solver uses.

The solution to c) could be 150 or 54 or 300

b) and c) could be clarified by the addition of parentheses:

b) as a)
c) as a) or (6 × 4) + (6 × 5)

The same rules apply when using parentheses for search queries. For example:

• women OR female AND "equal opportunities" OR discrimination

If the database deals with AND connectors before OR connectors, the result of this search may be quite unlike what the searcher intended. That is, female AND 'equal opportunities' would be solved first.

The addition of parentheses immediately solves the problem of ambiguity

• (women OR female) AND ("equal opportunities" OR discrimination)

Those parts of the query in parentheses will be dealt with first, followed by the remaining AND instruction. Figure 7.13 demonstrates the different results.

It can be helpful to say the search strings out loud to determine whether or not they are ambiguous.

How to combine terms in practice

Using the table or spider diagram of relevant terms, go through them, deciding how best to combine them so that all possibilities are covered. This may mean that a long list of search queries is created. Use of truncation and wildcards will reduce the numbers of queries.

If possible, keep queries relatively simple. This can be for two

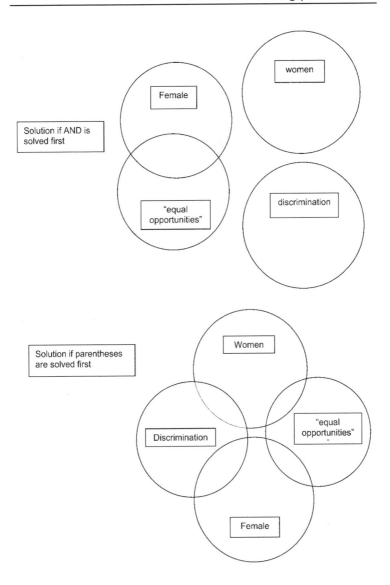

Figure 7.13 Search query using parentheses
Query: women OR female AND 'equal opportunities' OR discrimination

- long, complex search queries are liable to include errors
- use of a larger number of short search queries reduces the margin of error and allows the searcher to be flexible by combining previously run searches in different ways

For example, using the glass ceiling example above, the searcher may construct the following search strategies:

- "glass ceiling" AND (organi*atio? OR compan? OR institutio?) AND (UK OR "united kingdom")
- (EOC OR "equal opportunities commission") AND (wom*n OR femal?) AND workplace
- (EOC OR "equal opportunities commission") AND (wom*n OR femal?) AND promot?

where ? is used as a truncation symbol and * is used for a single character wildcard.

In order to include all the terms they wish, the searcher will have to construct a large number of complex search strings. It would be preferable, to run a larger number of simpler searches that can then be combined later, giving more flexibility. For example:

1. organi*atio? OR compan? OR institutio?
2. UK OR "united kingdom" OR british OR britain OR "great britain"
3. promot?
4. equal opportunit? OR "equal opportunies commission" OR EOC
5. discriminat?
6. wom*n OR femal?

giving sets 1 to 6 and so on.

The searcher can then combine searches in as many combinations as is required as shown in Table 7.4.

The resulting sets can be combined until the researcher is content that all appropriate combinations have been included.

Some of these less complex searches may result in very large numbers of results, which at first seem unmanageable. However,

Table 7.4 Combined searches

Combined searches	Set number
1) AND 2)	7
3) AND 4)	8
5) AND 6)	9
3) AND 6)	10
set 7 AND set 8 AND set 9	11
1) AND 5)	12

when these results are combined with others using an AND connector, the numbers will diminish because use of this operator has the effect of narrowing down the search.

The functions of the database(s) selected will dictate the exact method of combining the searches.

Step 5: Combining terms 2 (using other connectors)

Depending on the database(s) selected, additional connectors may be available. Use of these allows adaptation and focusing of the search so that the retrieved records are relevant and a manageable number. These devices are called proximity operators or connectors. Details of phrase searching may be included with the instructions for proximity connectors. The options usually comprise one or more of the following:

- terms within the same sentence or paragraph
- terms within a specified number of words of each other
- terms in a specified order (but not necessarily adjacent)

Terms within the same sentence or paragraph

If terms appear within the same sentence or paragraph, there is more likelihood that they have some relevance to each other. This is particularly true when searching the full texts of documents. If an AND search is selected, one term may appear near the beginning of the text and the other, not included until somewhere near the end. To achieve increased relevance, specify documents where the terms are used in close proximity so they are likely to have some relation to each other. To search for terms within the same sentence (in no particular order) use a connector such as /s

For example:

- slang /s french

and for terms within the same paragraph use /p
For example:

- slang /p dialect

Each database should be checked for the methods of doing this.

Terms within a specified number of words of each other

Databases vary in how they require the command for this instruction. The connector will retrieve records with the terms within a specified proximity of each other, but not usually in any particular order. For example:

- bridge within 6 span

or

- bridge /6 span

The records retrieved may include phrases such as:

- The Sydney Harbour Bridge has a span of . . .
- The span of any bridge that is built . . .

Another method of achieving a similar result is using the NEAR connector. As with all other connectors, databases should be checked for the options available and the means of executing them. It is up to the discretion of the searcher to select the number for the proximity of the terms.

Terms in a specified order

The option to specify that terms should be in a particular order (but not necessarily adjacent) may be available. This might be achieved by using the connectors BEFORE or AFTER. For example:

- gin BEFORE tonic
- C AFTER hepatitis

A variation of this, is being able to specify one word preceding another within the same sentence or same paragraph, by incorporating operators, for example +s (for preceding within the same sentence) or +p (for preceding within the same paragraph).

When to run the search

Having selected the relevant database(s) to use (see Chapter 6), it is at this point that the search is run. The search can be planned up to step four then additional connectors used to refine the results. Although it may seem a large amount of work, the planning process will save time and frustration as the searcher can be confident of having covered the most relevant terms and has a record of the process, making any revisions a straightforward procedure.

Evaluating the results

It is vital at every stage of the search that the retrieved records are investigated for relevance. By doing this the searcher can be sure they are finding the records they require. Criteria for evaluation should include:

- numbers of records retrieved
- position and frequency of the keywords used for the search (search terms are usually highlighted within retrieved records)
- inclusion of homographs, unintended truncated words and other irrelevant results

- additional relevant terms not included in the search strategy
- types of document retrieved
- any factors that may be limited in a future search (for example, date of publication, language)
- checking for related terms and relevant indexing terms or descriptors
- level of writing
- overall relevance of the subject matter to the work being undertaken

Use the information gleaned to modify and improve the search strategy.

Evaluation can take two forms:

1. quick scanning to check that the results are what was expected
2. in depth evaluation to identify records that will be saved and later followed up to find the full text

Quick scanning can be used when retrieving large numbers of records. The evaluation will move towards becoming more in depth as the search begins to focus on fewer, more relevant records.

The amount of records that constitute a 'manageable number' is a personal preference. To determine the maximum number of results that the searcher is aiming to retrieve, they should ask themselves, 'how many records would I be prepared to read in detail?' At an estimate, this would be around 20 to 40 records at a time.

Saving the results

Once a manageable number of relevant records has been achieved, save those which are deemed useful for the project. Not only should the records be saved, but also the search strategy and history so that the search can be re-run and/or the searches already performed, easily checked.

See Chapters 6 and 14 regarding saving searches and records, and managing the results of searches.

Completion of the search

When relevant records that have already been retrieved appear and no new records are being pulled up, the searcher can conclude that, for the present, the search is complete. New records are constantly being added to databases so it is important that during the course of the project, previously run searches are updated. As the research progresses, more terms may be encountered that should be included in search strategies, so new search queries will be devised using these terms.

Key points

- Plan and formulate a search strategy before embarking on a search using a structured database
- Searching is an iterative and heuristic process
- Do not cut corners or leave too little time
- Incorporate Boolean and other connectors as well as devices such as truncation and wildcards to focus the search and retrieve relevant records
- Set limits on the search or use the NOT connector to ignore extraneous records
- Evaluate the results at each stage using what is found to modify and improve the search strategy
- The aim of the search is to retrieve a manageable number of relevant results
- Save relevant records so that the information necessary for acquiring the full text is available
- Experience and careful evaluation of the records retrieved will help the improvement of searching techniques

---

● 8

CITATION SEARCHING

Chapter outline

- What is citation searching and why is it important?
- Citation indexes
- When to stop
- Electronic citation searching
- Problems associated with citation searching
- Cross referencing

What is citation searching and why is it important?

Having obtained a published work to support the research, the genealogy of the selected work is of importance when researching a topic thoroughly. Citation searching is similar to creating a family tree in finding who begat whom or, at least, which work influenced another. It is carried out in tandem with database and other searches.

Citation searching works on the basis of who cited whom in their work. This means that it is a case of working backwards and forwards in time to find where a particular work has been cited:

- Working backwards in time: following up the citations given in the article
- Working forwards in time: finding out where the article has been cited

Figure 8.1 shows how related works link by their references. It also demonstrates the complexity of the task. Imagine how Work 11 is discovered: this might be achieved by finding the reference made to it in Work 2. Work 12 may only be discovered by following the trail via Work B.

Citation searching is a process of finding works that are related, sometimes closely, by discovering those an author used (and referenced) when writing their own.

The reasons for performing a citation search

There are many reasons why a researcher may perform a citation search such as:

- finding the original work(s) on which an idea or research is based
- finding reactions to a work
- finding works that are closely related
- finding authors working in a similar field
- following up further developments in that field
- retrieving information about corrections or retractions of published work
- mapping trends in research
- identifying emerging research areas
- finding the frequency and the publications where works have been cited
- finding the impact of one author's work on others'
- finding the effect of research
- finding the influence of research on innovation, particularly when searching citations in a patent
- finding background information in a chosen topic
- when experiencing difficulties in discovering works using subject keyword searching

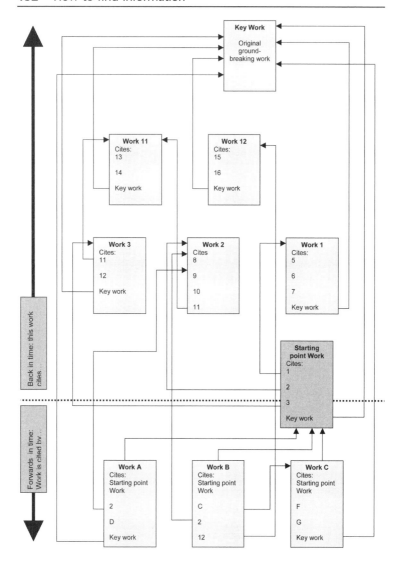

Figure 8.1 Citation search

Lawrence et al. argue that citation indexing also improves communication (Lawrence, Giles and Bollacker 1999: 67).

Citation indexes

A citation index is a record of cited references, usually in the form of a published list or an electronic database. For example, the *Current Law Case Citator* lists all English court cases that have been reported since 1947 as well as subsequent cases which have made reference to the case in question. For those working in other fields, the *ISI Web of Knowledge (WoK)* database provides 3 indexes:

* Arts and humanities citation index
* Science citation index
* Social science citation index

In order to proceed with a citation search, one (or more) work should be selected to act as the starting point. It is preferable that this work is highly relevant to the subject matter so that any other works retrieved by the search are also likely to be relevant.

The nature of citation searching means that amongst the items of interest retrieved, there will inevitably be works that are not relevant, or are of peripheral interest. It is therefore important that the information need is clearly defined together with the limits of the investigations (see Chapter 5) so that it can easily be decided whether or not an item is relevant.

Comprehensive citation searching including working forwards in time is difficult without a citation index.

When to stop

Citation searching can be a fascinating process, particularly when tracking developments in a chosen area. However, it is remarkably easy to find oneself following lines of investigation that are well beyond the scope of the original research. It can also be a time-consuming process, and the researcher needs to be able to draw a halt to the proceedings, although, as more information is uncovered as the research progresses, a return to citation searching may be necessary. The signals for reaching the limits of a citation search are:

- the works that are being retrieved have already been discovered in the search
- the works being discovered are becoming less and less relevant

Electronic citation searching

Online citation searching is a powerful tool for the researcher. It allows easy searching of records that have been cited in the selected document as well as those which have later cited that document. The *Web of Knowledge* Citation Indexes have the facility for citation searches (using the Cited Reference Search option), beginning on the *Lookup* page, using a combination of all or some of three fields:

- cited author
- cited work (that is, journal title, book title or patent number)
- cited year (the year the cited work was published; most effective when used in conjunction with the other search options)

For example, a search on the *WoK Lookup* page using the author name Cartwright, M. and the year the cited was published set as 1999 and 2000 results in six hits, one of which has a link to a record stored on the *WoK* database. The article reference is:
Cartwright, M. and Shepperd, M. (2000) An empirical investigation of an object-oriented software system. *IEEE Transactions on Software Engineering*, 26 (8): 786–796, August.

Clicking on the link to this article then gives two figures in the full record:

- Cited references: 19
- Times cited: 5

'Cited references' indicates the number of references that Cartwright and Shepperd included in their article. 'Times cited' indicates the number of subsequent articles that have cited Cartwright and Shepperd's article. Of the 19 cited references, 7 of them have records on *WoK* and therefore links to those records. All 5 of the 'times cited' records have links. The cited references date from 1988 to 1998 and the 'times cited' records from May 2002 to April 2003 (as at July 2003), demonstrating the backward- and forward-looking nature of citation searching.

From this point, the cited references and 'times cited' information on any of the linked documents can be viewed. A chain of related records can then be retrieved, by continuing to view references in each subsequent document, but beware becoming lost and moving into irrelevant territory along the way.

Science Direct allows i) a search for articles that have since been published and which have cited the selected document (*Cited By* search) and ii) an e-mail citation alerting service for notification when a document citing the selected one is added to the database. The results are limited to articles that are included in *Science Direct*. Another facility on this database is the ability to search the references field to discover where a particular author has been cited in articles on *Science Direct*.

Exactly what is retrieved using an online citation search depends on the database and the subscription. It may be possible to retrieve the full text (as on *Science Direct*), a citation with abstract or the basic citation of the document. If an item is linked using *CrossRef* the searcher may be able to access the full text of the item (see Chapter 11).

Using an electronic citation search allows a search for any of the authors of a work, not only the first author. However, only a limited number of databases provide a citation search facility.

Patent citations

The US Patent Office *Patent Full Text and Full Page Image* database[1] lists 'references cited' and also 'referenced by' information. The searcher is therefore able to retrieve records of subsequent patents that cite the selected patent and discover which patents the document has cited. The searcher may also search using the references field. The UK Patent Office does not currently offer this service.

Problems associated with citation searching

Although citation searching using an electronic database is easier than following up references using printed resources, it is not without its problems.

- Consider the case of using the *ISI Web of Knowledge* citation indexes. Performing the search is straightforward; however, the resulting records will be those that are held on the *WoK* database. Although a large and multidisciplinary database, it does not include all records of everything ever published and so many relevant records will not be included in the results.
- The inclusion of a citation in a document does not guarantee its quality. It should be evaluated like any other item (see Chapter 12).
- Bibliographic details of cited documents are provided by authors and any errors are transferred into the database.
- Any bias in the coverage of the database (for example, those aimed at the US) will be reflected in the citations included.
- There may be a limit on the date of coverage of the database. For example, WoS *Arts and Humanities Citation Index* has backfiles from 1975 but the *Science Citation Index Expanded* extends back to 1945.
- A search using an author's name may retrieve many results, some of which might be irrelevant because they refer to another author with the same surname (and possibly initial). Use information such as the date, affiliation and address to ascertain whether or not the author is the person intended.

One of the problems when performing a citation search is that of becoming lost in a long and convoluted trail of references. It is advisable to keep records of what has been discovered and where, so that the research trail does not become unmanageable or incomprehensible.

Cross referencing

Be organized when tracking down references discovered via a work. This may require use of a mixture of print and electronic resources. For example, a record retrieved on *Science Direct* comprises the bibliographic citation, the full text (for subscribers) and a list of references cited in the article. The references may be a mixture of those which contain no links at all, those that link to an abstract only and those that link to the full text of the article, including references. Those that contain no links at all will have to be traced using library catalogues and other methods (see Chapters 9 and 11).

When working with print resources, it is advisable to copy any pages of references and mark copies with details of where they were published. This will aid any further chasing up later.

Bibliographies, lists of references and footnotes should be used in order to cover the literature search comprehensively. It is this meticulous detective work that satisfies the researcher that they have been thorough.

British Standards

When searching for British Standards using the *British Standards Online* database[2], the information given includes cross references (with some hypertext links) to other standards. These references are all retrospective and do not include links to subsequent standards that have referred to the one currently being viewed. The standard itself may include a bibliography and a list of cross references, but again, it is retrospective information. The database does, however, allow a search using the expanded search page to discover which standards have replaced the selected standard. For example, searching using the standard number 6634 (BS 6634:1985, ISO 6954-1984, published in August 1985) retrieves BS ISO 6954:2000 published 16 years later in May 2001.

CrossRef

CrossRef is a collaborative development by a number of publishers which enables researchers to link directly from one article to another, regardless of publisher or publication. This is of immense benefit to the researcher who can easily follow up the references cited in an article.

Key points

- Citation searching is a means of investigating the influences on a work and the work it subsequently influenced
- A thorough search for information should include citation searching
- Keep to the defined scope of the research and do not become sidetracked
- Cross references should be checked for completeness

● 9

RESOURCE LOCATION

Chapter outline

- Introduction
- Locating items at the home institution
- Locating items not held in the home institution
- Searching the catalogues of other collections
- Other means of locating electronic materials
- Finding a commercial source of the material
- Other people
- Grey literature
- Other sources for locating materials

Introduction

Following resource discovery, the next step is to obtain the information that has been identified. This can be split into a two-stage process: resource location (dealt with in this chapter) and accessing those resources (see Chapter 11). Figure 9.1 shows how resource location forms the bridge between discovery and access.

Resource location is the process of identifying the whereabouts

Figure 9.1 Resource location as the bridge between discovery and access

of the full content (text, image, recording or other content) of the required information. There are many resources that allow the user to discover relevant items, for example abstract and indexing databases, library portals, electronic tables of contents and holdings catalogues. Sometimes the resource will allow immediate access to the full content. Often, though, the user is left to find the full content elsewhere. In this case it is necessary to know the options available and the decision will have to be taken concerning the most appropriate tool for the situation. The content may be hard copy or electronic (or both) and there are a number of possibilities for locating items. The choice of which to use will depend on:

- the format of the required content
- the permitted access to the resource (that is, selecting the most appropriate in the circumstances)
- balancing the time factor and the distance the researcher is prepared to travel to obtain the item
- whether the researcher is willing to spend money purchasing an item rather than borrowing it.

This chapter is concerned with searching collections for specific items that the researcher has identified via resource discovery. It also provides suggestions for and information about places to be investigated not only for locating materials, but for the discovery of sources (see Chapter 6).

Most resource location (and discovery) can be achieved by, say, scouring the catalogues of libraries and commercial suppliers and the lists of publications of organizations and so on. Other means may be necessary in certain circumstances where these tools are neither available nor appropriate. For example, it may be necessary to contact a small, private library by telephone or mail to find out if it stocks a certain item. Also, 'electronic records of manuscript and archive holdings are rare' (RSLG 2003: para. 63). This chapter is concerned mainly with the use of online location tools. Figure 9.2 illustrates the locations of resources and common tools to find the resource.

At this point in the search, the researcher should be in possession of full bibliographic or other descriptive details of the item(s) they require. Having this information will enable them to search the catalogues or other location tools for full content access.

The RSLG report (RSLG 2003: para. 42) includes the results of a survey which stated that '50 per cent of researchers think that their own university meets their research needs fairly well. 24 per cent think that their own university library meets their needs very well.' This is all well and good, but indicates that many researchers will be looking towards other sites for the supply of items they need. The RSLG has recommended a national strategy for the provision of research resources, led by a new strategic body, the Research Libraries Network. The remit of this body will include initiatives to improve and build on current work in the areas of resource discovery, location and access.

Resource location is not just about finding any provider that holds a copy of the required item. There is also the issue of finding the most appropriate copy. For example, the researcher may find that the British Library holds a copy of an item in its document supply catalogue. However, this is of no consequence if the user's own library provides immediate access to it.

Many libraries and other centres allow access to their catalogues (or OPACs) to search their holdings and find the status of items (see Chapter 2). New developments with OPACs are enabling users to search across other electronic resources that are linked to the catalogue interface.

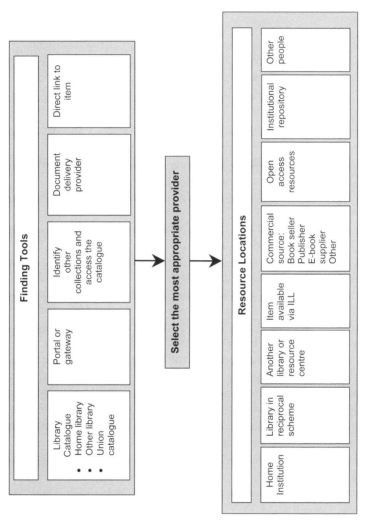

Figure 9.2 Resource location and finding tools

Locating items at the home institution

The home library is where the researcher holds the fullest membership, most likely the institution to which they are affiliated. If the researcher is a member of a university or other large institution, it is likely that first attempts at resource location will be made using their own library's OPAC. Those working at a distance to the home institution may wish to familiarize themselves with the catalogue of an information provider (such as a library or archive) at a more convenient location, but should be aware that there may be limits on the amount and types of materials that they can access (see Chapter 11).

The library catalogue is key to locating items, but there may be additional sources such as departmental collections or Web pages, or a special archive hidden away from the main collections. Some large institutions are multi-site and have libraries or information centres at each or at selected sites. Locating items may in this case be possible using a catalogue that covers all the libraries, or it may be necessary to use a number of different catalogues.

Locating items not held in the home institution

For high-level research, it is unlikely that any one library will provide access to all the items required. Be prepared to look further afield for information sources. If the details of a particular item cannot be found at the home institution:

- abandon the search and find an alternative source of similar information which is in stock
- turn to an interlibrary loan or document supply service (see Chapter 11)
- find an alternative location (either real or virtual) where the item is stored that will provide access to the item

It is this third option that will be dealt with here.

The options for resource location at an alternative location are:

- searching the catalogues of other collections

- locating another source of electronic materials
- finding a commercial source of the material
- using other people

These options will be dealt with in turn.

Searching the catalogues of other collections

Identifying collections

Before embarking on a search of another library, archive or information store, it is necessary to identify appropriate collections. Such collections might be those of research libraries, specialist collections, national libraries, private collections, museums, archives and so on. There will be some collections that will be obvious, for example, the national libraries and HE libraries. HERO provides information about and links to HE libraries (and other information sources) both in the UK and worldwide.

Others collections will be less well known. The *Aslib Directory of Information Sources in the United Kingdom* (Reynard 2002) is a comprehensive publication of many thousands of entries giving details of information collections and is a good starting point. Entries are alphabetical by organization and include those for institutes, commissions, associations and government bodies. There is also a cross-referenced subject index.

Collection descriptions

Collection descriptions are a means of users finding collections that are of interest to them. They often include information such as the holdings and collection strengths. They can be used for resource discovery as well as resource location. One example is the *Backstage*[1] performing arts gateway which allows the user to search for information about the locations of performing arts collections in the UK.

SCONE[2] (Scottish Collections Network Extension) provides

descriptions of collections held in Scottish libraries, museums and archives, and collections about Scottish topics held elsewhere. These descriptions can be searched by collection name and location, and by the names of associated persons and organizations including collectors, collection owners and administrators, and the subjects covered by the collections.

The *Archives Hub*[3] is a national gateway of descriptions of archive and manuscript collections held in UK HE and colleges. The site provides information about the collections with links directly to many sites for further information and catalogues.

Research libraries

When locating items at research libraries, always have a clear idea of whether or not access to those sources will be allowed (see Chapter 11).

Searching OPACs and other catalogues

OPACs are generally easily accessible via the Web. Locating items at libraries which do not have an OPAC is more problematic.

Union or merged catalogues

Union or merged catalogues are invaluable as they allow searches of multiple catalogues simultaneously, therefore saving time. They can be a means of locating resources from a wide range of libraries. There are a number of initiatives in the UK by various consortia. There is, as yet, no national union catalogue, although work is progressing in this area.

Serials Union Catalogue (SUNCAT)

The UK's pilot union catalogue of serials, SUNCAT[4] (Serials UNion CATalogue), provides a means of locating serials at a national level. The first phase of the project lasts until the end of

2004 and it is expected to continue for a further two years. It will be of great use to researchers as it will 'comprise records and holdings from the British Library, the National Libraries of Scotland and Wales, large university research university libraries, and some smaller, more specialist, institutions' (RSLP 2001).

Consortium of University Research Libraries (CURL) and COPAC

The members of CURL comprise over two dozen university and legal deposit libraries from around the UK and Ireland. One of the membership criteria for universities is those 'with a national or international reputation for scholarship and research information facilities' and those with 'extensive collections on a scale appropriate for the support of a broad range of research activity' (CURL 2003). The members of CURL acknowledge their standing as libraries with research collections that support the UK research community and they are committed to providing access to their holdings via their union catalogue and to their collections.

The CURL catalogue, COPAC, is freely available on the Web. Users are able to search simultaneously across the catalogues of the member libraries to retrieve a full catalogue record, details of the location(s) of holdings and, at some libraries, details of availability.

InforM25

The M25 consortium of HE libraries has created a virtual union catalogue of member institutions. The group comprises HE libraries in and around the London area. The InforM25 service enables simultaneous access to over 140 college and university library catalogues and a separate Union List of Serials[5] (ULS) of participating institutions. The user may search all catalogues, a selection from one of three zones: north, south or inner London or a combination of any individual selected catalogues. The ULS provides the means of searching serial holdings across the University of London and the University of Westminster libraries. The ULS offers more detailed information regarding serial holdings at participating institutions than the InforM25 union catalogue.

Riding

The Riding consortium[6] provides improved access to resources in two ways: a means of searching simultaneously the catalogues of member institutions; a reciprocal access and borrowing scheme. The consortium is based in Yorkshire, Humberside, and the North East of England.

SASCAT

The School of Advanced Study (SAS) of the University of London has a joint catalogue, SASCAT[7], which covers the holdings of the libraries of its seven members. The results of a search on the catalogue give the user the location of the material within the member libraries.

Scottish Confederation of University and Research Libraries (SCURL)

CAIRNS[8] (Co-operative Academic Information Retrieval Network for Scotland) is a union catalogue for 16 higher education and research institution libraries in Scotland (plus a handful of others) under the auspices of SCURL.

SALSER[9] is the union catalogue of serials held by members of SCURL. Users may search individual libraries, select groups by location or search the entire content of the catalogue.

Other means of locating electronic materials

There are many initiatives being developed to simplify access to electronic documents and other e-resources. Locating electronic items is not always an easy task: users should first check the holdings at their own institution and follow this by searching open access collections for which there is no union catalogue. Coupled with this, because it is a developing area, it is constantly changing. Library catalogues may link directly to major open access collections such as those mentioned in Chapter 6, but this is not yet universal. The means of locating (and accessing) open access journals using search engines such as *Google* is improving, although an institution's own or a discipline-focused **repository** provide better searching facilities.

e-journals

It is common for large proportions of a large library's journal collection to be electronic. Titles are usually listed, and may be linked to, on the catalogue along with the print titles. Although a library may not stock or provide access to a given title, there are collections of open access journals being created and added to. These are journals for which there is no charge to the user and which can be accessed via the Web (see also open access below). Researchers can check the contents of such collections to find out whether they include the item they wish to locate.

e-books

Currently the situation with e-books is confused. Libraries are purchasing titles which are being added to their catalogues, but titles from suppliers such as *ebrary*[10] that can be viewed freely are not being added. Locating a title can therefore be time consuming because of having to search a number of suppliers.

Open access

Access to scholarly information is an issue that is exercising many working at the cutting edge of research. Increasing numbers of institutions and researchers are joining the drive towards open access and freely available **e-prints**. The sciences and social sciences are currently more represented than the arts and humanities. For example, RePEc[11] is providing free access to large amounts of research documents in the area of economics including working papers and journal articles. This type of archive as a source for locating documents is valuable because of the ease of access to the material.

Susanne Dobratz and Birgit Matthaei (Dobratz 2003) have compiled a list of examples of gateways of open repositories in a number of subject areas:

- '*Medicine:* Behavioral and Brain Science Prints Interactive Archive, Cambridge University Press, United Kingdom
- *Economics:* RePec, Research Papers in Economics, United Kingdom
- *Mathematics:* Math-Net, University of Osnabrück, Germany
- *Physics:* PhysNet/PhysDoc, University of Oldenburg, Germany
- *Cognitive Science:* CogPrints, University of Southampton, United Kingdom
- *Psychology:* Psychology, University of Southampton, United Kingdom
- *Educational Sciences:* Education-line, University of Leeds, United Kingdom
- *Organic Agriculture:* Organic Eprints, Denmark
- *Philosophy:* Sammelpunkt. Elektronisch archivierte Theorie, Austria'

Other freely available materials

Although subscriptions or pay-per-view are required for much information, there are some providers that allow free access to their sources. One example is UK National Statistics which provides free access to data and publications.

Finding a commercial source of the material

The researcher may be prepared to purchase an item personally or have other sources of funding for purchase. In these cases they would wish to find a commercial source of the item.

Booksellers

For books a local book shop may suffice, although rare or out of print materials may prove more problematic. In these cases the services of a specialist book store or an out of print supplier such as *AbeBooks*[12] or *Bookfinder*[13] may be needed. Locating such items can be difficult.

Books can be located easily via a bookseller's own Web site (providing that it is in print). *Blackwell's*[14] is one of the larger companies in the UK which covers all major subject areas and has a number of outlets as well as an online service. Some of the smaller specialist booksellers publish their catalogues only in print. Others are large, purely online global concerns, for example, *Amazon*[15] which sells not only books, but audio visual and other items.

Journals and other resources

Journal articles and other document types may be available for pay-per-view delivery. The publisher's Web site or an online database can be used to locate such items.

Other people

Personal contacts such as colleagues or supervisors and discussion lists can be valuable means of locating information. Colleagues may not only know where items may be located, they may also be willing to lend personal copies of items (within copyright restrictions).

Grey literature

Locating grey literature can be a difficult and frustrating task. In the case of pamphlets, reports and leaflets it is likely that no library will stock them and they may not have a bibliographic description.

If an item is proving difficult to locate in a library, one solution can be to approach the company, individual or department directly. For example, if the researcher has the details of a thesis from another country that is proving difficult to locate using conventional methods, running a search on the WWW can result in finding contact details for the academic department from where it originated or even personal contact details of the author. Of course, this method is somewhat unreliable as people move on and details change, but it is possible that an individual might be willing to send copies of publications to the researcher.

Other sources for locating materials

EU information

Although much European Union information is freely available on the EU Web sites the researcher looking for other EU materials may find what they require at one of the 44 European Documentation Centres (EDCs) in the UK or one of the European Public Information Centres (EPICs). Details can be found on the *European Information Network in the UK*[16] Web site.

Newspapers

One of the problems for libraries of storing back copies of newspapers is the space that they take up and their physical shape, making storage and shelving (and consequently retrieval) difficult. To address these difficulties many libraries retain copies of newspapers in a microform format or via an electronic provider. The British Library's Newspaper Collection is the UK's major provider of back copies of newspapers, including national and provincial titles. There is a dedicated catalogue for this collection.

Official publications

The BOPCRIS database includes a collections directory to help users find the location of their chosen documents. The Public Record Office catalogue, PROCAT, allows users to search for documents and find the location of many in the UK. For example, the Hospital Records database shows where the records of individual hospitals are held and the A2A (Access to Archives) database provides access to other catalogues in England.

Historical records, archives and manuscripts

The UK National Register of Archives[17] (NRA) provides information about manuscripts and historical records relating to British history and their locations. It is maintained by the Historical Manuscripts Commission. The ARCHON directory gives contact and location details of the archives included in the NRA, including those that are not located in the UK.

AIM25[18] is being created to provide online access to collection level descriptions of the archives of over fifty higher education institutions and learned societies within the greater London area. It is under development and funded by the Research Support Libraries Programme (RSLP). Participating institutions include the University of London, other universities located within the M25 consortium of academic libraries and some of the royal colleges and societies of medicine and science in London. The details provided are similar to those of the Archives Hub. Areas of collection strengths include military and political papers, history of science, technology, medical science and education, literary papers and missionary records.

RSLP projects

The RSLP[19] ran a number of projects which aimed to make collection descriptions available in the humanities and social sciences (Research Collections in the Humanities and Social Sciences) and a number of Collaborative Collection Management projects. Its Web site provides links to the individual projects. Subjects include:

- company reports
- research resources in Wales
- archaeology resources
- nineteenth-century pamphlet collections

Although funding has ended, many of the projects provide ongoing services.

Key points

- Resource location is about finding the most appropriate source of information
- Search catalogues including union catalogues
- Open access materials might be linked to library catalogues, but may need searching separately
- The location of items, especially grey literature, may involve using printed catalogues and contacting people personally as well as online searching

---

10

USING THE WORLD WIDE WEB FOR RESEARCH

Chapter outline

- Introduction
- Means of locating information on the WWW
- Accessing the selected site
- Subject gateways
- Using search engines
- Evaluating information found on the WWW
- Some useful tips

Introduction

The World Wide Web (WWW or Web) forms only one part of the Internet. The Internet is a multiplex of networks comprising elements such as:

- e-mail
- discussion groups and newsgroups
- the WWW
- a means of file transfer

This chapter deals with the WWW part of the Internet, the freely available resources it contains and locating and evaluating those resources. The WWW provides access to text documents, graphics, moving images and hyperlinks leading to further information.

Unlike some other publishing processes, items on the WWW may be published without review or any other editorial procedure. This means that the quality and reliability of the material can be questionable. It is the user's responsibility to ensure that any information used is of a suitable quality. To this end, it is advisable to become proficient in Web evaluation techniques and not an indiscriminate Web user.

The WWW is undoubtedly a valuable research tool. There is a large amount of high-quality information freely available: there is also much dubious material. The skill lies in distinguishing between the two.

It is likely that an answer to a query can be found on the Web. It may also be true that information can be found much quicker simply by picking up a printed source close to hand. The choice of source can be dependent on a number of factors:

- location: proximity where does the user physically have to be to access the information
- time: the time taken either to log on to a computer or obtain the hard copy to access the information
- currency: although Web sources can be kept up to date easily, this does not always happen in practice

The most appropriate choice is that which is most convenient and relevant to the current query and situation.

Means of locating information on the WWW

The information required may be located on the Web using one or more of a selection of different location tools. The options are:

- typing the URL in the address box
- using a gateway or portal

- using a search engine

The choice of which will depend on whether the researcher would like to access:

1. a specific Web site where the URL is known
2. a specific Web site where the URL is unknown
3. a Web site on a chosen topic that has been selected by a specialist
4. a selection of Web sites on a chosen topic
5. a relevant Web site from no particular provider or source

Where a URL is known, the researcher can easily type in the address to access the site. For options 2 and 5, a search engine would be a suitable solution. Options 3, 4 and 5 could make the use of a gateway or directory.

One can make an educated guess at the URL of certain Web sites if the precise address is unknown. Commonly used formats of URL contain elements such as:

- .com or .co.uk for a commercial company
- .ac.uk or .edu for higher education sites (respectively in the UK and the US)
- .gov.uk for UK government sites
- .org for other organizations such as professional bodies or charities

An abbreviation at the end of the URL can indicate a country for example .fr for France or .de for Germany.

Accessing the selected site

Once the selected or a relevant site has been found, access to it may or may not be straightforward. Sites will fall into one or more of the following categories:

- 'Freely available – the resource is free of charge, with no restrictions on access

- Conditionally free – the resource (or part of it) is freely available under certain conditions' (JISC 2003a). The conditions might relate to the institution or require registration.
- 'Institutional subscription – the resource (or part of it) can be accessed only if your institution holds a subscription/licence' (JISC 2003a). This may mean that access is only available from computers at a specified location such as those at certain institutions such as a university or company.

Conditions of access may limit usage to a specified number of concurrent users. Some sites provide limited access, perhaps by way of a guest user's option which allows access to some, but not all of the resource.

Subject gateways

Internet gateways are subject-based collections of online information sources located at external sites. They often take the form of a directory and have usually been selected and evaluated by a subject specialist or information professional.

A hub is a cluster of subject gateways and usually covers a broad subject area such as social science or engineering. Both gateways and hubs may have an integral search facility for finding resources in their collection. The examples of gateways and hubs given here have been created with academic users as their target audience although freely available to anyone.

The RDN in the UK provides hubs in main subject areas:

- ALTIS – Hospitality, Leisure, Sport and Tourism
- Artifact – Arts and Creative Industries
- BIOME – Health and Life Sciences
- EEVL – Engineering, Mathematics and Computing
- GEsource – Geography and Environment
- Humbul – Humanities
- PSIgate – Physical Sciences
- SOSIG – Social Sciences, Business and Law

The user can drill down to the topic they require using the browse facility, search each hub or search all hubs using the search facility on the RDN home page.

BUBL is a multidisciplinary information service that lists selected Web sites in major subject categories. Users may search the whole site, limit the numbers of results using the 5 : 15 service or find sites using the directory.

Portals

A portal is a refined gateway which can be personalized and customized according to the user's status and preferences. They may include features such as the ability to cross-search multiple databases, the use of personalized alerting services and the ability to select the resources included. They often include means for resource discovery, e-mail access and online discussion. Some probe deeper than others (sometimes known as thick portals) and may, for example, allow users to link directly to the full text of a journal article provided by a supplier such as *Ingenta* rather than merely linking to the main search page (Dolphin, Miller and Sherratt 2002). A gateway is static in that it appears the same to all users.

The JISC describes a portal as a 'possibly personalised, common point of access where searching can be carried out across one or more than one resource and the amalgamated results viewed' (JISC 2004a). The JISC Subject Portals Project is developing portal functionality for five of the RDN hubs.

Using search engines

What is a search engine?

The WWW is a conglomeration of diverse information with no imposed order, indexing or system of storage. This means that, unlike a well-ordered library where all items are catalogued, classified and shelved in a logical order, finding relevant documents on the WWW can feel like searching for a needle in a haystack, one which is vast and growing rapidly.

A search engine is a device for locating Internet sites based on criteria input by the user. They are usually freely available, although some require a subscription (for example, *Northern Light*[1]). Although each engine would have the user believe that it is the best and covers most, if not all, of the Web, the reality is somewhat different. Most Web searchers have a favourite engine and it is difficult to break the habit of using that engine without considering any others.

The search engines considered here are those designed to search the general WWW rather than those that search within a particular Web site.

Numbers of search engines

Searchers can generally name a handful of well-known search engines. In fact, there are many hundreds freely available. They differ in their methods of searching, the amount of the Web they cover, how they display the results and other features. It is worth comparing engines and the searcher should be prepared to use a selection if they do not retrieve the results they require.

Features of search engines

Methods of locating information

The two main types of search method are i) engines that allow the user to type in a query and ii) those that work on a directory basis, allowing the user to drill down through categories to reach the desired site. The directory option is constructed by human beings who determine the most appropriate category for each site.

i) Engines that allow the user to type in a query

Within this category there are variants:

- free text search

- assisted search
- natural language search

Free text searching allows the user to input the query using a command-box or similar. The user can be highly specific and incorporate Boolean search terms and other operators. For the expert searcher, this can be the most reliable and satisfying means of searching. Examples of engines that include this option are *Alta Vista*[2] and *All the Web*[3].

An assisted search provides boxes for the user to complete. These might be to find:

- all the words
- any of the words
- the exact phrase

and are in fact using Boolean logic (see Chapter 7).

Natural language searching allows the user to input the query as if they were asking a verbal question. For example the search query might be 'Why did Henry the Eighth execute Anne Boleyn?' or 'How can I access the Library of Congress catalogue?' One of the most popular natural language search engines is *Ask Jeeves*[4], but there are also others such as *Answer Bus*[5] which allows input in a number of different European languages.

ii) Directories

Directory or index search engines work using a hierarchical system of subjects. The subject can be focused until the exact topic is found. For example, *Yahoo UK*[6] lists around 14 topics including government, health, regional and science. Clicking on the government link leads to a page containing:

'Top categories:

- UK Local Government
- UK National Government
- Irish Local Government
- Irish National Government

Additional categories:

- Business to Business
- Documents
- Embassies and Consulates (258) (The figures following each category indicate the numbers of sites included within that category)
- Law (2683)
- Politics (11422)
- Public and Civil Service (9)
- Research Labs (24)
- Statistics (48)'

and links to specific sites such as the 10 Downing Street site, UK Online government portal and the Government of Ireland.

Directories are useful when the searcher wants a selection of sites about a particular topic, for example, music therapy. But for sites that include specific text anywhere on the page, a free text engine is preferable. Some engines are hybrids and offer both options.

Meta search engines

Meta or multi-search engines (sometimes called meta crawlers) provide the means of searching across a number of engines in one operation. It is a useful method of spreading the search over a wider area of the Web. For example, the *Ixquick*[7] search engine can search up to 12 engines (including *Alta Vista, Ask Jeeves, Lycos* and *Gigablast*). A search results in a list of retrieved hits, each showing on which engine it was found, and the ranking of the site on that engine. *Kartoo*[8] searches around 14 engines and selects some for the search, although the user can opt for a search covering all the engines.

A drawback of such engines is that truncation and wildcard characters are unlikely to be identical on all the engines used for the search.

Targeted engines

Some engines are designed to be either country such as *Lycos Français*[9] or the Finnish engine *www.fi*[10].

Quick and advanced search options

Many of the larger search engines have both quick and advanced (or 'more precision') search options. The quick search is useful when using a small number of search terms or phrase(s) and when the researcher is not too concerned about the numbers or relevance of the results. If the search term is an unusual word or a phrase, the quick search can be an easy method of obtaining relevant results. It may be possible to use Boolean operators, wildcards or phrase marks in the quick search box for increased precision.

The advanced search option allows for more precision in the results and increased relevance. It may allow features such as selecting the language of the results or searching for selected domains or types of document such as PDF. For example, a phrase search performed using the *Google UK*[11] search engine (pages from the UK) resulted in the following:

Quick search:

• Query: 'internal combustion engine'
• Numbers of results: 6720

Advanced search:

• Query: 'internal combustion engine'
• Language limit: English
• Format limit: Adobe Acrobat PDF
• Date limit: Pages updated in the last three months
• Occurrences: Return pages where the terms appear in the title
• Numbers of results: 68

Default settings

When typing in two or more search terms the searcher should be aware of the default setting of the engine, whether it is a Boolean

AND or OR. The results will differ depending on the setting. This information is usually given in the 'Help' function of the engine. Always check the help function to be assured that the results are what were expected and to take advantage of the engine's features.

Interface

The interfaces of search engines vary: some have text and graphics in every available inch of space, whilst others are cleaner looking. Some have moving images, such as advertisers' promotional material, whilst others include no obvious commercial material. Home pages vary from those that easily fit into a window to those that require much scrolling to view the entire page. It may be possible to customize the view if there is a *My search engine* option such as that on *Yahoo*. Customizing allows the searcher to select the areas that are displayed, retaining only the parts that are of interest, and may include an alerting facility. Preferences are a matter for the individual.

The advanced search option may not be obvious if the link is in tiny text as on *All the Web* and *Yahoo*.

An engine such as *Kartoo* has an interesting method of displaying results by providing a pictorial representation (although a typical list format is also available). This is a diagram of how the selected sites link to each other by topic. The results interface also provides a list of topics, allowing the searcher to narrow down their search by defining relevant topics. *Kartoo* also provides a basic search history facility for each query.

Comparing the results

The results pages of search engines vary as much as the home pages. Results are displayed in different orders, with varying amounts of information for evaluation of the results and with differing 'busyness' of display.

Relevance and ranking of results

Probably the criterion that is of paramount importance to the researcher is that of the relevance of the results retrieved. The ranking can be important if there are many hits as it is unlikely that the searcher will trawl through all the results.

Engine designers are constantly attempting to improve search mechanisms so that the results displayed have high relevance. This does, of course, depend on the search query input by the searcher. There are factors such as where in the page the terms appear (a result is likely to be more relevant if the term is in the title), the metadata (hidden data that describes the page) and the engine's ability to counter any scurrilous tricks attempted by Web page publishers to make their page rank highest (such as including terms in the smallest possible font, typed repeatedly, and cunningly disguised by using the same colour text as the background).

Ranking depends on the search engines' perception of how relevant a page is. Again, the engines differ in how they achieve this.

The results page

The results page displays short extracts designed to enable assessment of whether or not a site is relevant and needs further investigation. They vary in the amount of information they provide and some have additional features such as 'related search' links or *Alta Vista* providing the date when the site was last refreshed and its list of terms for refining the search. Such features can make the search easier and more relevant, for example, *Google* provides a 'search within results' option to help narrow down the search. *Teoma*[12] offers a number of options to refine the search plus links to additional resources. *Vivisimo*[13] sorts the results into groups or 'clusters' (Vivisimo 2004) of related resources.

Reliability of search engines

Many search engines will retrieve hits quickly and with a high degree of relevance. However, there are some issues of which the searcher should be aware. For example, some engines construct their databases using a spider or Web crawler. The crawler wanders around the WWW gathering sites as it goes. This may take some time, which means that a lot can change between one visit from the spider and the next as the average age of the pages on some major engines varies from four weeks old to six months.

The estimated number of indexed pages on each engine varies wildly. For example, *Google* claims to index more than 4.3 billion Web pages (claimed by Google at 22 February 2004), *All the Web*, over 3 billion pages (claimed at the same date), *Teoma*, 1.5 billion and *AltaVista*, 1 billion (2 September 2003 figures taken from *SearchEngineWatch*) (Sullivan 2003). These are approximate estimates of the numbers of effective pages and there are many issues that affect the calculation of size. The size of an engine's indexing may matter to the searcher if they are trying to find information as Greg Notess suggests in *SearchEngineShowdown* (Notess 2003), such as the name of a person, an usual term, or checking for plagiarism. Not all will retrieve certain types of files such as PDF documents. See the invisible Web below.

The directories of directory search engines are compiled by humans. This means that the user's opinion of where a site may be listed may not match that of the directory compiler. For example, on the Yahoo.com directory, geography is listed under social sciences rather than humanities.

The invisible Web

The vast numbers of pages indexed by search engines or added to directories can engender a false sense of security for the searcher. In fact, there are large parts of the WWW which are not easily accessed by engines which have been called the invisible Web. Sites that may be included in this category could be:

- password-protected pages
- documents in PDF or other formats
- URLs with no other links leading to them

There are attempts to rectify the inaccessibility of some invisible sites. Since 2001, *Google* has included Adobe PDF documents in its searches. This was a major step forward for researchers as many scholarly publications are produced in this format.

IncyWincy[14] is an example of an engine attempting to retrieve sites which would otherwise be difficult to access.

Selecting an engine

There is such a choice of engines on offer with many variables between engines, that it is understandable why many searchers remain faithful to one particular favourite. Some searches will benefit from being run on a subject or country specific engine. For example, *Scirus*[15] is a science-specific search engine (from the publishers, Elsevier) and Phil Bradley lists a collection of country specific engines (Bradley 2004). Although the engine selected remains the preference of the researcher, some criteria for choosing a type of search engine are those given in Table 10.1. If one search engine does not produce suitable results, it is worth re-running the search on another.

Finding out more about search engines

There are sites designed to help the user find out more about using search engines and provide interesting comparison statistics (although not always obtained using rigorous scientific methods)

- Phil Bradley's Web pages (Bradley 2004)
- Greg Notess' site SearchEngineShowdown (Notess 2003)
- *SearchEngineWatch* from Danny Sullivan (Sullivan 2003)

Evaluating information found on the WWW

Because documents retrieved on the WWW are such a mixture of quality ranging from the scholarly and reliable to the

Table 10.1 Some criteria for selecting search engines

Task	Type of engine
Searcher has prepared key terms	Free text
Searcher knows of a specific site they wish to access	Free text
Searcher wishes to seek terms within the text	Free text
Searcher wishes to use a number of key terms including synonyms	Free text
Searcher wishes to input multiple terms but is unsure of connectors	Assisted free text
Searcher wishes to input the query as a question	Natural language
Searcher wishes to browse a topic	Directory/Index (or Gateway)
Searcher wishes to obtain an overview of sites in a subject area	Directory/Index (or Gateway)
Searcher wishes to perform as wide a search as possible	Meta engine
Searcher is concerned with sites from a specific country	Country specific (or Gateway)
Searcher is concerned with sites in a particular subject area	Subject specific (or Gateway)
Sites may form part of the invisible Web	PDF compliant, invisible Web engine (or Gateway)

untrustworthy, researchers should equip themselves with strategies for evaluating the content they discover. Some sites are obviously designed for commercial purposes or are overtly lighthearted. Others can be more difficult to ascertain whether they are reliable scholarly information sources or if there is a hidden agenda or include unreliable claims.

Work through the criteria for each site under consideration. If unsure about the quality of a site, ignore it or make it quite clear that the information is unsupported or questionable.

Criteria for evaluating Web sites

Web sites may be evaluated using the following criteria:

- Ownership: Sites which do not make this information clear should not be trusted. The author could be anybody. Although corporate owners can be biased, their intentions are usually clear.
- Authority: If the user cannot trust the author or the corporate body who published the site, then they should not use the information.
- Currency: a site that is no longer being updated, including the hyperlinks, should not be trusted. The information may be incorrect.
- Quality of content: Judging quality can be difficult, especially in pages that appear plausible. On closer inspection the searcher may find there are no supporting data for opinions or facts. Content can be biased in a number of ways (as in any publication), for example, political, academic (that is, supporting only one school of thought), commercial and so on.
- Intended audience: Information should be at the right level.

The criteria can be judged by the searcher considering the following questions:

Ownership

1. Is it clear who is the author of the site/page?
2. Is there a corporate owner of the information?
3. Are there contact details for the page owner?

Authority

1. What authority does the author possess?
2. Was the searcher made aware of the site from a reliable source?

Currency

1. How up to date is the information?
2. Are the Web links on the page working?

Quality of content

1. Are claims supported by reliable evidence?
2. What is the quality of the use of language and grammar?
3. Do Web links lead to high-quality and reliable sites?
4. Is the information biased in any way?

Intended audience

1. Who is the intended audience?
2. Is the site a vehicle for commercial promotional material?
3. Does the site include advertising?
4. Are you being asked for money?
5. See also Chapter 12

The main point is to be critical.

Some useful tips

Expert use of the WWW takes practice and also a willingness to become aware of the issues and options available. The following list contains some helpful hints that make using the WWW more efficient:

- To find the terms searched for on a Web page use the computer's find function. This may be in the Edit menu or there might be a hot key/shortcut such as using Control Key + F. This function can save scrolling down a long page.
- Many major engines provide a 'search within' function to narrow down a search without re-running it. This enables searching of the retrieved results.
- Bookmarking a site (or adding a site to a list of favourites) is a useful option when the searcher wishes to return to the site at

a later time. When returning to a site using this method, refresh or reload the page to ensure that the latest version is displayed.

Key points

- Gateways are a means of quickly finding relevant and usually trustworthy information
- Search engines vary in their features, presentation and relevance ranking
- Be prepared to use more than a single search engine
- Information found on the WWW should be evaluated for reliability

---

11

ACCESSING MATERIALS

Chapter outline

- Introduction
- Accessing physical materials held at the home institution
- e-resources available via the home institution
- Using other libraries
- Document delivery services
- Access to scholarly publications
- Digital Object Identifiers (DOI)
- Accessing other sources of information

Introduction

By this stage of the information-seeking process the researcher will have the full details of the item (whether physical or electronic) and its location (if not being obtained using an interlibrary loan service).

There are many issues related to the access of items such as:

- borrowing rights
- subscriptions and authentication for use of electronic resources

- viewing, saving and printing electronic items
- restrictions on use of materials obtained from other libraries
- initiatives such as open access
- entitlement and cost of interlibrary loans/document supply
- potential difficulties in accessing grey literature
- agreements between publishers regarding direct access from a database to full text
- sensitive information
- time delays

Accessing physical materials held at the home institution

The researcher's primary source is likely to be the home institution. For those working at a distance, another source may prove more convenient, but the home site is the one that will provide access to subscription electronic resources (at least, those subscribed to by the institution) and may offer the most comprehensive borrowing rights. There may be a special arrangement for distance learners to enable them to obtain resources from the home library (see Chapter 2).

The researcher will have borrowing and access rights agreed by their institution and, for the most part, will be able to access materials at no personal cost. They should become proficient in using their own library's catalogue so that they can be sure whether or not an item is in stock and not waste time attempting to access it elsewhere.

Some libraries are multi-site and the user might have to make special arrangements to obtain items from sister sites. For example, there may be a regular delivery service of items requested from other sites such as remote stores.

Closed access libraries require that the user request the item(s) and then wait for them to be fetched by a member of library staff. There is a time factor involved here which should be taken into account when planning the research and requesting such items.

Even at the home institution there may be items that are designated restricted access or held in a closed access store. Special arrangements for access then have to be made.

e-resources available via the home institution

Links from databases to full text

Depending on publishers and licensing agreements, users can increasingly access the full text of an item directly from a bibliographic database. Some databases such as *Science Direct* or *Ebsco Online* are stores of full text articles which the searcher is able to discover by running a search on the database. They can then access the full text if they either have appropriate authentication or are willing to pay using a credit card for direct document delivery.

Links to full text rely on the subscriber's entitlements. As the electronic environment grows, more agreements and options are being put into place as publishers and database providers negotiate deals and libraries provide links using their own catalogues. *ISI* WoK, for example, offers two additional services for HE:

- *Holdings*: links from *WoK* to the library's own catalogue. If the catalogue includes any linked URLs of electronic titles subscribed to by the library the user may access these titles even if they are not the subject of an agreement between ISI and the publisher.
- *ISI Links:* links directly from *WoK* full records to the online full text (where it exists). The links are controlled by the institution and reflect the institution's entitlements. This service requires an agreement between ISI and the publisher providing the full text.

Issues related to electronic provision of materials

It is usual to be able to save, print and e-mail and/or fax items. Users may not be able to copy text in a document that is in PDF. There may be a choice of full text format such as HTML (Hypertext Markup Language) or PDF.

One of the difficulties with electronic resources is the different methods of proceeding from discovery of the resource to obtaining the item in full. The simplest method is to find the required resource, click on a link and have the full item presented with no interim stages. However, having found the details of the required item it may then be necessary to transfer to a separate resource from another provider with a different interface to access the full text.

As stated earlier, the transition from resource discovery, via resource location to the full text is becoming increasingly seamless, with access possible from one resource to another without any interim steps.

e-books

Many institutions are offering some book titles electronically. At present, there are a number of different methods of achieving this and decisions have to be taken regarding which suppliers to use (they vary in their methods of provision), which access mechanism to adopt (via PC (Personal Computer) or hand-held device) and how details should be incorporated on the library catalogue. e-book suppliers such as *ebrary* offer users free access to view the full text of titles on-screen, others require the library to purchase virtual copies. The future developments in the area of e-books are at present, uncertain (Lynch 2001).

There are many e-book titles that are available freely such as those listed on *Project Gutenberg*[1]. Titles tend to be older publications, no longer in copyright.

Using other libraries

As the UK moves towards a co-ordinated approach for research support, there are more arrangements for reciprocal access and borrowing between university libraries. If the home library does not stock the item required, it might be obtained at an institution where there is a reciprocal access and/or borrowing agreement. This may be a local, regional or national arrangement. A researcher wishing to take advantage of this type of arrangement must first search the appropriate library or union catalogue to check holdings.

The SCONUL (Society of College, National and University

Libraries) Research Extra[2] scheme allows research students and academic staff to access and borrow items from other participating libraries (currently most UK HE institutions). Users should be aware that electronic resources are not included in the scheme. SCONUL also promotes other access and borrowing schemes.

Examples of reciprocal schemes between institutions and other local or associated institutions include the RIDING schemes arranged by a consortium of universities in Yorkshire and Humberside and that arranged in Scotland between the libraries of Glasgow, Strathclyde, Glasgow Caledonian and Paisley Universities.

National libraries allow researchers to use their resources for the purposes of research, although there may be some restrictions. The British Library will issue a reader's pass to a researcher, but they must have exhausted all other sources of the information and be able to demonstrate a 'legitimate need to use the items in the collection' (British Library 2004) for their research. There may be access restrictions on rare materials with special conservation requirements such as those at the National Library of Scotland.

When considering using any reciprocal scheme, the researcher should first check the libraries that are currently participating in a scheme and any restrictions on access and borrowing imposed by those libraries. Some collections may be valuable or rare and access might only be allowed to those who are deemed eligible.

Document delivery services

For ILL many libraries use the British Library's Document Supply Centre (BLDSC), run from Boston Spa in Yorkshire. This offers a number of different services to which registered users have access. It is a separate service to that of the British Library at St. Pancras in London.

A journal article requested via interlibrary loan is usually provided as a photocopy that the user may keep. If the researcher has requested more than one article from a single issue of a journal, then the whole issue will be loaned in order to comply with copyright law. Copies of book chapters can sometimes be supplied (dependent on copyright) otherwise the entire volume is supplied. Allowable usage of items may vary depending on restrictions set by the owner of the item. For example, an item may be restricted to library use only: the borrower may not be able to take the item out of the library which arranged the interlibrary loan. Books can be borrowed for a set period and renewal might not be extended. Heavy penalties are incurred if ILL items are not returned by the given date.

When requesting an item via interlibrary loan and signing the copyright declaration the user is agreeing to use the item in compliance with the terms of the copyright agreement, for example, use only for personal research or not having been previously supplied with the same item. A library can acquire items via interlibrary loan for multiple users, but a higher, copyright cleared fee is charged.

The most common formats of interlibrary loan are books or articles, but the user may find that they are sent a microform, particularly if a thesis has been requested. The usage instructions on these items should be read carefully as there may be guidelines regarding printing and other instructions.

Although a photocopy of a journal article obtained from the British Library may be delivered within a few days, some take longer to arrive. Sometimes the British Library does not possess the item that has been requested. In such a case, there may be a delay while it obtains the item. Delays may also occur if an item is in heavy demand and a waiting list has developed or it is being obtained from abroad. In any case, requesting an item via interlibrary loan will result in having to wait to obtain the item and the research should be planned around this.

Document supply services can be used to locate and access documents. The British Library[3] catalogue has a separate search option ('document supply material only') for items it is able to supply remotely. Services such as *Ingenta* (the online or fax/ariel articles options) and *DocDel*[4] provide online document delivery, but charge for this service and the British Library provides a subscription document delivery service, *Inside. DocDel* also delivers via post and fax as well as online. A directory of document suppliers is maintained by *DocDel.net*. A separate index lists suppliers in main subject areas and a list of UK suppliers: many provide a search facility of their database of documents. If an item is located on an e-journal database, yet the institution does not subscribe to that title, it might still be obtainable by paying personally for document delivery (if provided) by credit card. Journal publishers sometimes offer a pay-per-view document delivery service such as that provided by the scientific publisher, Kluwer[5] or Elsevier STM publishers via their *Science Direct*[6] service or by a supplier such as Ebsco.

Access to scholarly publications

In learned institutions around the UK and globally, researchers are creating records of their work including articles, datasets, first drafts of papers and so on. There is a wealth of information locked away which, if made available to other researchers, could substantially change the culture and speed of research developments. The opening up of access to scholarly publications is being developed globally.

The e-print revolution

The e-print revolution started in 1991 with a computer system for storing and providing access to scholarly papers. This repository[7] (now at Cornell University) is known as *arXiv* and the content is in the disciplines of physics, mathematics, non-linear science and computer science. Papers can be submitted when the author chooses (which can be immediately upon completion) and once in the archive, are open access, that is, freely available to users.

An e-print can be described as a scholarly publication in electronic form. The content could be a research or conference paper, the results of experiments or other research. They are either pre-prints (that is prior to being refereed) or post-prints (peer-reviewed items). These electronic papers may be stored in an e-print repository or archive, and their electronic nature allows for more rapid dissemination than the traditional route of publishing.

The JISC in the UK has funded a number of projects (for example, ePrints UK) investigating access to institutional resources as part of its FAIR (Focus on Access to Institutional Resources) programme. These include projects concerned with 'fostering the creation of institutional e-print repositories within the UK' and 'the development of new types of services that provide some kind of unified access to the content of such repositories' (Day 2003). E-print repositories are becoming increasingly common as part of an institution's archive of research information (Day 2003).

Documents relating to research prior to publication are of great value to researchers. Although some would not wish their work to be available either in an early draft or before being reviewed (particularly in the medical sciences), there are many who value the opportunity for others to access such publications. Academic documents such as these are usually available at no cost to the user: the impact of the work is one of the greatest benefits for the author.

The results of this literature being freed up is that researchers will have immediate access to a larger corpus of research literature. As Theo Andrew stated, 'individual scholars, seeing an opportunity to distribute their work easily to a potentially wide audience and, as a by-product, raise their research profiles, have also seized the opportunity to use new technology by posting research material online' (Andrew 2003).

Institutional repositories

Since the development and availability of free e-print software, universities are developing internal repositories for self-archived (that is, deposited by the author) items of research output. This action can free up publications, certainly within the institution, but, by complying with OAI (Open Archives Initiative) protocol and allowing external access, can release findings to the global research community, therefore raising the impact of the publication. These repositories may contain diverse items including e-prints, data, conference papers, working drafts and other grey literature as well as video, maps, musical compositions and other resources.

Issues related to the 'disclosure and sharing of content' (JISC 2004b), for example those of intellectual property rights, are being investigated by projects under the JISC FAIR programme. Institutional repositories may or may not be open access: some sections may be limited to small groups. Institutions developing e-print repositories include those at St. Andrews[8], Nottingham[9] and Glasgow[10] universities.

Other repositories

Some repositories are those dedicated to a single discipline such as the *arXiv* physics repository. The *Chemistry Preprint Server*[11] provides free access to chemistry literature submitted by researchers and closely follows the *arXiv* model. The resources may be fully prepared articles or work in progress.

A major e-print resource for scientists and engineers based in the US is the *E-print Network*[12] which provides the means of searching for e-prints in these disciplines.

Another model is that of networked repositories such as the DARE (Digital Academic Repositories)[13] initiative of the Dutch universities.

The Open Archive Initiative

The OAI[14] (Open Archive Initiative) is promoted by those committed to the increased dissemination of scholarly materials including information users, providers and brokers/mediators. It focuses on the technological framework and protocols required to make this possible, rather than the content or economic issues of scholarly communication. The OAI promotes sharing of content, compliance with the OAI protocol and the development of an international network of institutional repositories.

OAI compliant e-print repositories ease access to their content which can be used by anyone (Simpson 2002). Repositories that comply with the OAI protocol now amount to over one hundred, dispersed around the world. Major centres include:

- *arXiv* (see above)
- *BioMed Central*[15]
- *Directory of Open Access Journals* (DOAJ)[16]
- *Public Library of Science* (PLoS)[17]
- *PubMed*[18] and *PubMed Central*[19]

BioMed Central

BioMed Central is a provider of free access, peer-reviewed bio-medical research literature. This UK based publisher encourages the creation of new open access journals and offers publication services to research groups.

The Directory of Open Access Journals

The DOAJ was created by Lund University Libraries. It contains information about the journals which are listed on its database, and links to the full text of many of the journals from the DOAJ site. There are hundreds of journals included and the content is growing. The subject coverage is in the fields of science, human sciences and humanities and papers are either peer-reviewed or editorially controlled to retain quality. The DOAJ's definition of an open access journal is one that uses 'a funding model that does not charge readers or their institutions for access' (DOAJ 2003).

The Public Library of Science (PLoS)

PLoS is a not-for-profit organization that is working towards making scientific and medical literature open access. Its goals include providing 'unlimited access to the latest scientific research' and to 'facilitate research, informed medical practice, and education by making it possible to freely search the full text of every published article' (PLoS 2003). Users may use the material for any lawful purpose including downloading, distributing and linking to the full text. The authors have the right to retain control over the integrity of their work and the right to be correctly acknowledged and cited.

PLoS is publishing journals (PLoS Biology first issued October 2003 and PLoS Medicine mid-2004) to which users have free access. There are plans to publish further titles, all of which will be peer-reviewed and freely available. Authors (or their institutions) are however, required to pay to offset publishing costs.

PubMed and PubMed Central

PubMed contains citations of articles in the field of biomedical science including links to many in full text. *PubMed Central* (PMC) is a full text archive of journals in the life sciences from the US National Library of Medicine. PMC is running a digitization programme to add non-electronic back issues to the archive.

Digital Object Identifiers (DOI)

Electronic publications have the advantage that any citations can link directly to the (electronic) full text of the work referenced. However, the inclusion of links may cause difficulties for both author and reader. One problem lies in the ephemeral and transient nature of the Internet. URLs change, links become broken or redundant and the reader is no longer able to find or access the documents to which the author refers.

The problem can be solved by the use of DOIs which provide a specific identifier for the document and therefore a more reliable and persistent means of providing access to electronic references. This method is being used, although it is invisible to the reader, for example, when accessing a document using *CrossRef* (as used in *ISI Web of Knowledge* database) which links from the citation of the document to the full text.

DOIs can alert the user to a more recent version of the document and be used in situations where the issue of intellectual property is involved: it 'could be used to identify the agreements and parties involved' (Paskin 2003).

Accessing other sources of information

Grey literature

SIGLE

Access to SIGLE, the European grey literature database of multi-disciplinary sciences, is via the STN International interface (Web access) or on CD-ROM. *STNEasy*[20] is the scientific and technical information network database. There is a charge for some of the services available from *STN Easy*. Signing up for a single user online account is free, but there is a charge for searching.

GrayLIT Network

The GrayLIT[21] Network provides online access to US Government grey literature including that of the Defence Technical Information Center (DTIC), Department of Energy (DOE), Environmental Protection Agency (EPA) and the space agency, NASA.

Theses and dissertations

Doctoral theses are usually available to anybody who wishes to read them (although some have restricted access owing to sensitive content). Some confidential works may be accessed with special permission from the author or other persons. In the UK doctoral theses not supplied by the home institution can be accessed via the British Library's British Thesis Service[22]. The item will be supplied in microform. If the British Library does not hold the full text, there will be a delay while they obtain the original document for microfilming from the originating institution. Obtaining the full text of overseas items may be difficult, or at the very least, take some time.

Electronic Theses and Dissertations (ETD)

Increasing numbers of higher education institutions are providing full-text open access to their own theses and dissertations electronically, although the UK has lagged behind developments in the US and Australia. It is commonly believed that a national approach is likely to be the most successful solution for the UK as there will be a co-ordinated solution for technical issues (see Chapter 17).

Networked Digital Library of Theses and Dissertations (NDLTD)

This repository[23] has over 180 members mainly in the US, but also from Canada, the UK and other countries. The British Library is a member institution as are the national libraries of Australia, Canada and Portugal as well as some universities. The aim of the NDLTD is to improve 'graduate education by developing accessible digital libraries of theses and dissertations' (NDLTD 2003). Information about items is provided by member institutions, not by their authors, and results in a union catalogue of ETDs. The Web site provides links to other sites with ETDs which are not members of the NDLTD.

Australian Digital Theses (ADT)

The Australian Digital Theses programme provides a 'national collaborative distributed database of digitised theses produced at Australian Universities' (ADT 2003). It includes entries of research theses (PhD and Masters by Research) with full bibliographic information, an abstract and links to the full text. The member institutions are all Australian universities. Theses eligible for deposit are those passed by a participating institution.

Official publications

Official documents may include items such as government committee reports. The BOPCRIS database provides full text access to a limited number of the documents.

HMSO (Her Majesty's Stationery Office) 'encourages access to public sector information' (HMSO 2003) and provides online access to UK legislation, the IAR (Information Asset Register), command papers, London, Edinburgh and Belfast Gazettes (full access is a subscription service).

TSO (The Stationery Office) is the commercial (and separate) publishing branch of HMSO which was privatized in 1996. Publications include the UKOP (UK Official Publications) catalogue.

The Public Record Office (PRO) Documents Online service provides access to digitized public records. Although searching is free, downloading an image is a chargeable service.

Datasets

Many datasets require a subscription, particularly maps and spatial data. Others such as the UK Data Archive[24] (UKDA) provides free access to digital data in the social sciences and humanities to anyone in UK HE. It also incorporates two other data services, *Qualidata* (social science qualitative datasets) and the *History Data Service*.

UK National Statistics provides free online access to many economic and socio-economic time series datasets, statistics and National Statistics publications.

The National Geophysical Data Center[25] provides links to world data centres in the areas of geography, glaciology, geology, geophysics and so on. Specialist knowledge may be needed for access to the correct data in a useable format.

Conference literature

Conference proceedings and pre-prints are often published by the society or academic body which organized the conference and may be available via that body for a charge. Many conference proceedings are made available on the WWW, some free and some as a charged service.

Standards and patents

Many large libraries stock standards and patents relevant to their users either in print or online. The status of items (whether they are current or have been superseded) can be checked using online services.

Images and sound

Institutions may subscribe to collections of images such as the Education Image Gallery and Education Media OnLine[26] hosted by Edina. Other services include the National Sound Archive from the British Library or those listed at the AHRB Centre for British Film and Television Studies[27]. Materials will not necessarily be stored in a digital format.

Archives

Accessing archive materials such as local history, council, genealogical or planning records could take some dedication as the only available source may be the original copy. Once the item has been located, the user may have to make a special journey to access it.

Company information

It can be difficult to find the details and to access reports or marketing information from industry. Much of this information is either commercially sensitive or not in the public domain. Libraries might hold marketing information such as that published by Mintel or a company reports database. Such information is usually expensive.

Key points

- Leave enough time to find a means of accessing items not available immediately at the home library
- Explore all possibilities of accessing materials from the home institution including reciprocal access and borrowing schemes

---

12

EVALUATION OF RESOURCES

Chapter outline

- The importance of evaluation
- Criteria for evaluation

The importance of evaluation

Analysis of the problem and definition of the information need will have laid the foundations for the evaluation of resources. During the research process the researcher will encounter much more information than they will use, and they will have to select or reject what they find in order to build a relevant reserve for the project. The process of selection will be governed by evaluation. Any resource that is selected must have been chosen for its relevance: any that are irrelevant should be rejected.

The question 'Is this resource relevant to the project?' should be considered for every item that is encountered. For some resources it is obvious they are irrelevant, but for others, it is not so straightforward.

The process of evaluation takes place throughout the research process as resources are discovered, located and accessed. All types of resources should be evaluated for relevance, whatever their length or format, that is, whether it is the citation, abstract or full text of a document, a photograph, list of data or government report.

Practical considerations

Citations or bibliographic descriptions

Citations and bibliographic descriptions can be difficult to evaluate for relevance because so little information is included. Additional information may be required to judge some items. This could mean accessing publisher's information or obtaining the full text in order to facilitate a more informed decision.

Abstracts and summaries

Abstracts and summaries are excellent for assessing validity and relevance. They are short enough to be read quickly and, providing they are well written, include key points in a succinct and meaningful manner.

Full content

The researcher will not have the time nor the inclination to read the entire content of every full text resource, such as books or articles, they encounter. They therefore have four options:

- to read any given abstract or summary. In the case of a book, this might be the introduction, the information on the back cover or that supplied by a publisher.
- to read any headings or tables of contents.
- to scan the document. This is a skill in itself and takes some practice.
- to look carefully at any diagrams or tables that are included in the item as they give much information in an easily digested form.

For many items, evaluation is a two stage process. If selected using, say, only a citation, the researcher should have the evaluation criteria in mind when reading the full text.

Criteria for evaluation

Like the evaluation of a Web site (see Chapter 10), there are a number of criteria that should be considered when attempting to evaluate a resource:

- Provenance: author; authority; reputation; publisher
- Content: level; composition; accuracy; comprehensiveness; currency; bias; substantiality; uniqueness; validity; intended audience; writing and language; organization
- Relation to the subject: importance of work; comparison with other sources
- Access and use: availability; accessibility; time-scale; permissions; format

Table 12.1 lists questions that should be considered when evaluating a resource. The researcher should consider those that have some bearing on the item under scrutiny. A decision about relevance can be taken fairly quickly, depending on the responses.

Key points

- Every item should be tested with the question 'Is this resource relevant to the project?'
- The evaluation can take the form of a series of pertinent questions

---

Table 12.1 Evaluation of resources: points to consider

Provenance	
Author	Who is the author?
	What are the author's qualifications, reputation or credentials?
	Does the author have any affiliation with a recognized body or institution?
	Is the author a recognized expert in the subject area?
	Is the author cited by other experts in the subject?
	If there is no named author(s), from where does the item originate?
Authority	Has the resource been peer-reviewed, refereed or edited?
	Has the resource been sponsored in any way or validated by a recognized authority (perhaps in a foreword)?
	Are any references to the resource from reputable sources?
	Have the details been obtained from a reliable source?
Publisher	Is the publisher a recognized academic publisher or other recognized source?
	If not, what is their reputation?
Content	
Accuracy	Where possible, check the accuracy of the content
	Are spelling, diagrams and typesetting accurate?
Bias	What is/are the reason(s) for publication? For example, extending knowledge or commercial?
	Is there any obvious or more subtle bias: political, commercial or otherwise?
	Is there any evidence of commercial sponsorship?
Comparisons	Does the resource duplicate material from other sources?
	If so, which sources should be retained and which rejected?
	Does the author repeat material written by others?
	Does the resource include research methods or design similar to those being used by the researcher?

Composition	Are there any indexing terms, descriptors, keywords or subject headings to describe the content?
	Is the resource a primary or secondary source?
Comprehensiveness	Have any topics or elements been omitted?
	Does the resource achieve its stated purpose?
	Does the content match the abstract or table of contents?
	Does the content meet the claims of the author or abstract?
	Is there too much/too little detail?
	Is the coverage too broad/too narrow?
	Does the research topic form the main topic or a peripheral topic?
Currency	What is the date of publication?
	There may be some time between conception and publication. Is the resource still valid?
	If the content is historical, is it relevant?
Intended audience	At whom is the resource mainly aimed?
	Is the level too simplistic/too complex?
Organization	Is the division of chapters and sections useful to the reader?
	Do any headings make sense?
	Do diagrams or illustrations enhance the text?
	Are diagrams, illustrations and tables placed in close proximity to relevant text, avoiding awkward page turns?
	Is the title meaningful and does it reflect the content?
	Does the resource contain additional information such as further reading or information about related materials?
	Are the layout and typesetting clear and easy to use?
	Are sections an appropriate length for ease of use?
	Is the system of numbering or headings useful to the user?
	Is the index comprehensive?
Substance	What is the tone of the content?
	Does it have seriousness and gravitas?
	Is it significant?
Uniqueness	Can the information be obtained elsewhere?

	Does the resource contain ground-breaking research or other original work?
	Is the resource a unique primary source?
Validity	Is the work based on sound research?
	Are references and a bibliography included?
	Are any citations from reputable sources?
	Is there reliable evidence to support any claims or results of investigations?
	Is any data used gathered from reliable sources?
Use of language	Are explanations clear?
	Is the sentence construction confused or too verbose?
	What is the style of writing: academic, informal?
	Is the text grammatically correct?
	Are any technical terms, acronyms or other unusual terms explained?

Relation to the subject

Comparisons	Does the content support or oppose other subject specialists?
Publication	If an article, what is the journal's impact factor rating?
Significance	Is the resource a significant work in the subject area?
	Have other respected authors in the subject field made reference to the work?

Access and use

Availability	Does the complete item exist?
	If so, where?
Accessibility	Is the content accessible by the researcher?
	If it is accessible, is it available in time for the researcher's needs?
Format	Is the resource in a format that is acceptable to the researcher?
	Is it clear what the format will be (from bibliographic or descriptive details)?
	Is the resource available in multiple formats?
	What is the country of origin of the resource?
	In what language is the full text (this may differ to the bibliographic details)?

	If the language is one not used by the researcher, is a translation available?
	Will the country of origin have any bearing on the content (for example, bias)?
Permissions	Is any special permission required to access or use the resource?
	Can copyright and other permissions be obtained in time?
	Is it clear who should be contacted to obtain any permissions?

Overall judgement

Does the resource comply with the criteria set when delimiting the area of research?

13

CITING REFERENCES

Chapter outline

- Terminology
- The purpose of citing references
- Citation and reference styles

Terminology

The following terms are often confused and sometimes used interchangeably:

- Citation: quotation of or inspiration derived from a passage, book or author in support of an argument. The citation appears in the body of the text. All citations should be included in the list of references.
- References: a list of sources cited (referred to) in the text.
- Bibliography: a list of sources consulted but not cited and other relevant or interesting sources or a list of sources by a particular author or on a specified subject.
- Further reading: additional sources that may be of interest to the reader. Used instead of, not as well as, a bibliography.

- Footnote: a note given at the foot of a page referring to something on that page. Usually indicated by a figure or letter.
- Endnote: a note given at the end of a chapter or at the end of the text referring to something within that chapter or text. Usually indicated by a figure or letter.

References to publications are used:

1. for citation searching and finding other articles of interest
2. when citing authors/publications in one's own work

The author should always give the citation of any work when it is referred to in the text. When composing references there are some points to note:

- There are a number of different styles of referencing (see below)
- The author should select the preferred style of any body or person for whom they are writing (such as a publisher or academic department)
- There are set pieces of information that should be included
- Consistency is paramount
- The author should ensure that all punctuation and typefaces are correct
- Use of bibliographic software aids consistency and accuracy (see Chapter 14)

The purpose of citing references

Any work such as a doctoral thesis, a company report or an article is likely to have been influenced by the work of others, building on existing knowledge to form new arguments or to critique or compare views. Some require a review of the literature in order to:

- demonstrate knowledge and an understanding of the subject
- demonstrate an awareness of works and authors that have been instrumental in the development of, or provide meaningful comment on, the subject

- provide a framework for the remainder of the dissertation or thesis

Other pieces of work can be primarily vehicles to demonstrate knowledge or are a résumé of the subject.

Whatever the case, the researcher should give full acknowledgement to the works or ideas of others referred to in the text:

a) so that the reader is assured that the work is based on or influenced by other reputable work
b) so that the reader can follow up any references of interest
c) as evidence of other's work that has been used to formulate the conclusions
d) to avoid unsubstantiated claims
e) to avoid plagiarism (see Chapter 15)

Citation and reference styles

The main consideration with style is to be consistent. Once a style has been selected, the author should adhere to it unfailingly. Care should be taken with accuracy of referencing, both the information included and how it is presented.

The author should check any existing guidelines and take care to follow them if writing as part of an award bearing course, for a publisher or a conference paper, or any other situation.

Citing within the text

Citations within the text may be a passing reference or a direct quotation from an author. They may focus on either the author or the idea (Sharp, Peters and Howard 2002: 202).

- Focus on the author: Fleming (1928) proved that . . .
- Focus on the idea: The staphylococci are unable to grow because of the presence of the mould (Fleming 1928)

Elements of a reference

A reference has fixed elements (BSI 1989: 3) which should be included for accuracy and fullness of information. The elements vary according to the format of the work or item being referenced but can be universally expressed by the following:

- Originator: author, artist, composer, editor, inventor, official body or organization
- Title of the individual item: a book, article, Web page and so on
- Format (when necessary)
- New version or replacement information: edition number, revised version, and in the case of Web pages, the date it was accessed
- Place of origin
- Publisher/owner
- Date of publication or creation
- Identifier or number: volume and issue number; number in a series; URL; page number(s)
- Title of work or series in which the item is contained: title of the journal, title of book or map series

Other elements might also be included depending on the item being referenced, such as the scale of a map, the language used for a computer program or details of a foreign language or translation.

How to obtain the information to be included

The information included in the reference should be obtained directly from the item, for example, the reverse of the title page of a book or on any container. Other sources might include publisher's materials or other catalogues.

Style

There are numerous styles of referencing, the two most common being Harvard and numeric (or Vancouver). As far as the author is concerned, the main advantage of using a style such as Harvard is that it is easier to manage when making amendments to the text, because the order of the list of references does not change (they are alphabetical rather than in the order that they appear in the body text). Others prefer numeric styles for being less intrusive in the text.

Even within a set style, there are variants such as use of bold text, italics or underlining to highlight an element, differences in capitalization, or the exact punctuation used. Information given on how to cite references should be considered as guidance, and the author should use their discretion for the exact details. However, some publishers or organizations expect precise styles. Authors should consult guidance on citation styles that have been supplied before submitting a manuscript.

Harvard style

As far as can be ascertained, there is no one definitive Harvard style. The citation should include the surname of the author being quoted or referred to and the year of the publication being cited. For example:

- (Rumsey 2004)

If the author's name appears in the body text, the year is given in brackets. For example:

- Rumsey (2004) suggests that . . .

Depending on the selected style, page numbers may be included. For example:

- Rumsey (2004, pp.11–13)

The references are listed in alphabetical order of author. References by the same author written in the same year, should append an extra letter, a, b and so on. For example, Rumsey (1999a) and Rumsey (1999b). These letters should also be included in the reference list.

Numeric or Vancouver style

The numeric style operates by each citation being allotted a number in sequence. In this way, the first citation the reader encounters in a document is number one, the second number two and so on. The list of references is therefore created using the order that the citations appear in the text. If a citation is used a second or subsequent time, it is assigned the original number. The number of the citation in the text may be given in brackets or superscript, for example:

- The school of thought that Freud [23] developed was...
- The school of thought that Freud[23] developed was...

In the list of references, the author's name may be given in the order: first name, last name rather than the other way round because the reader finds the reference using the allotted numbers, not the name.

Footnotes and endnotes

A method that is generally less common is that of incorporating references as footnotes. However, the legal community uses this method and, in addition, often gathers together the cases cited in a text in a list at the end. It can be argued that the use of footnotes is intrusive to the flow of the text. The footnote appears at the bottom of the page on which it is referred.

Other styles

Other styles are often a variation on the two main models of Harvard or numeric. Accepted styles can vary by discipline or professional body. Some in common use are those used by the IEEE, the APA and the MLA (Modern Languages Association).

Electronic resources and other formats

Items other than books or journal articles can prove difficult to reference, particularly government publications and electronic resources such as Web sites. Each set style usually offers guidance in this area but that often does not solve queries such as defining the author of a Web site. There are numerous models for citing electronic resources such as those listed by IFLA (International Federation of Library Associations and Institutions) (IFLA 2003).

Citing References: a user's guide (Fisher and Hanstock 2003) gives the following model for citing Web sites in Harvard format:

AUTHOR or EDITOR, year. Title [online]. Place of publication: Publisher. Available at: <URL> [Accessed Date].

The author can be the same as the publisher which may be a large organization. It is important not to be confused between the author/publisher (who creates the intellectual content of the site) and the webmaster (who is concerned with the technical maintenance of the site). If page numbers are not given on the resource, then they cannot be included in the reference (although paragraph or chapter numbers may be an alternative if included in the text).

The URL of the resource should be included and the date it was accessed and enough detail given for any reader to find the item (providing it is still in existence). For any problematic item, the writer should remain consistent and refer to any guidelines that are appropriate such as those provided by Fisher and Hanstock, any other suitable guide or a relevant professional body.

Abbreviations of titles

Within references, accepted abbreviations are often used for the titles of journals or other publications. These should only be used if they are accepted by the publication and authors should take care that they use the correct abbreviation as some publications use the same letters, or similar abbreviations can easily be confused. For example JCB can be used for:

- Journal of Commercial Bank Lending
- Journal of Contemporary Business
- Journal of Creative Behavior
- Jurisprudence Commerciale de Bruxelles
- Kansas Judicial Council Bulletin

Similar abbreviations:

- Ann Biol   Annales Biologiques
- Ann Biol An   Annales de Biologie Animale, Bio-
                            chimie, et Biophysique
- Ann Biol Cl   Annales de Biologie Clinique (Paris)
- Ann Biol (Copenhagen) Annales Biologiques (Copenhagen)

(taken from *Periodical Title Abbreviations*, Alkire 2003)

A publication such as *Periodical Title Abbreviations* should be used to find accepted abbreviations (Alkire 2003).

Legal journals and law reports use abbreviations extensively. There are publications dedicated to listing legal abbreviations including Raistrick's book (Raistrick 1993) and Cardiff University Law Library's online database (Law Library 2003).

Other abbreviations

Other abbreviations that might be encountered are as follows:

- Ibid. (itself an abbreviation of *ibidem* and sometimes further abbreviated to ib.) means 'in the same book or passage' (as the one quoted immediately before it). Often confused with op. cit. (see below).
- Op. cit. (*opere citato*) means 'in the work already quoted' and refers the reader to a previous citation. It is therefore necessary to include the author's name in the citation.
- Et al. (*et allii*: and others) is used when an item has three or more authors or creators.

Key points

- Always reference a work when it is cited in the text, whether quoted directly or as a passing reference
- Be consistent in reference style
- Use the correct style for the situation
- Make sure the content and the typesetting of the references is accurate

14

KEEPING RECORDS

Chapter outline

- Efficient searching and well-ordered records
- Maintaining records of searches
- Saving records and details of works accessed
- Bibliographic software

Efficient searching and well-ordered records

Earlier chapters have already advocated the need for organized preparation and information seeking. Well-ordered records and processes make the management and use of information a straightforward and painless process. There will be occasions when incomplete records or other problems arise, but if the researcher is able to start from a logically constructed and managed base, the whole process should save time, wasted effort and frustration.

The complexity and methods of information storage and record-keeping will depend largely on the size of the project. It is not worth spending time (and possibly money) setting up a complex bibliographic software system for a short piece of work. For a large-scale project such as a PhD thesis, the effort would be worthwhile, especially if undertaken at the outset of the work.

Maintaining records of searches

The researcher who has prepared their search strategy (see Chapter 7) will have records of the searches they intend to run. The results of those searches and follow-up tactics resulting from the success or otherwise may differ from the original plan:

- some searches may have produced too few or too many results
- alternative terms may have been discovered prompting additional searches
- the searcher may have access to additional resources, for example, if the library subscribes to a new database

In order to ensure that the researcher does not waste time rerunning searches already performed, or is able to check back and re-run previously run searches to gather updates, records of searches should be maintained.

To do this there are a number of options, including written and electronic solutions. Some may like to jot down the searches carried out and the results in a notebook or other safe place. Others might prefer an electronic solution such as a word processed document, spreadsheet or database. The advantages of electronic solutions are that records can be sorted for ease of reference and the results printed out if required, perhaps as part of an assessed assignment. Whatever the format, the information will include:

- search terms
- source (such as the name of the database or index used)
- date on which the search was run (or edited)
- numbers of results
- relevance of results
- notes for future searches
- numbering of each search for ease (if using a database, this may be essential)

For example, an entry in a search log for a researcher working in the topic area of perception and the developing child may include entries such as those in Table 14.1.

Printouts of search histories (see below) may be adequate, but additional information such as the date the search was run should be added.

Saving searches and search histories

The search history created when running searches on a database can be printed out for reference. As mentioned in Chapter 6, some online databases allow the user to save their searches and search histories for later reference or editing during a future session.

Saving records and details of works accessed

Saving individual records is vital for:

- creating a complete reference list and for citing references
- following up references
- creating a databank of references in a particular subject for future use

Many online databases allow the user to save, print or download records (see Chapter 6).

Whatever the task, the researcher should keep full and accurate records of works and bibliographic records that have been accessed. A hastily scribbled quotation or a photocopied page that does not contain work details is often impossible to track down later on. Another trap is that of noting the author and title of a chapter that forms a chapter of a book, but failing to keep a record of the editor and title of the book itself.

All too often it is when the work is drawing to a close and a deadline is looming that the researcher realizes they do not have the full details for the list of references. Panic then ensues, and they either have to hope that luck prevails or that the item in

Table 14.1 Example of a word-processed record of searches

No	Search terms	Source	Date	Limits	Nos of results	Relevance	Notes
1	(Infant or child* or toddler or baby or babies) AND (perception OR perceive)	Web of Knowledge	15.6.04	L = English J	5471	Mixed	Needs refining. Meaning of word perception
2	(aural OR audio) AND (perception OR perceive)	Web of Knowledge	15.6.04	L = English J	281	High	
3	(Infant or child* or toddler or baby or babies) AND (perception OR perceive)	PsycINFO	20.6.04	D = from 1990 L = English J	386	Mixed	Needs refining. Meaning of word perception
4	(aural OR audio) AND (perception OR perceive)	PsycINFO	20.6.04	D = from 1990 L = English J	18	High	Some language references
5	aural perception	ZETOC	19.1.04	None	18	High	
6	Author name: Hollier M P	Ingenta	19.1.04	None	5	High	

Limits:
D = date of publication
L = language
J = journal articles

question can be recovered using an electronic search. If a reference cannot be traced, they may have to remove it.

Bibliographic software

Bibliographic software (or reference management software) is designed to allow users to store, manage and use references. There are a number of commercial systems on the market and many academic establishments provide use of one or more packages for their members.

The software provides functions such as:

- allowing the user to download references directly to the database from bibliographic databases such as *Web of Knowledge*
- manipulation of the data in order to format the references into the correct bibliographic style (such as Harvard)
- linking the citation in the text with the reference at the end
- enabling easy creation and formatting of a list of references
- providing a means of building a personal library of references

However, these benefits do come at a price. First, there is the monetary cost of the software if it is not being provided by an institution or organization. Second, setting up the software to one's personal preferences requires time and skill. Therefore, it is only advisable to use this software if the project warrants it or if the user intends to continue to build a personal library. Once it has been set up, it is straightforward to run and can save much time and effort. Creating the list of references in this way also eliminates errors in formatting such as incorrect punctuation or typographical errors when re-typing (providing, of course that the formatting is set up correctly and the original text bears no mistakes). It is also a convenient means of storing a large collection of references.

For those online bibliographic databases that are set up to import references to bibliographic software, the process of adding references is quick and straightforward. For some, it is necessary to deal with filters which can be a complex issue and users should read the product's instructions carefully. However, not all online bibliographic databases are designed to enable the user to download references directly into a bibliographic software package. There may be an option to save the results as a text file which can then be imported into the bibliographic database. The imported references may need some editing.

Some packages are available for PDA (Personal Digital Assistant) computers (and, of course, can be used on laptops) which researchers may find useful when roaming. Being able to add references, even manually, whilst on the move can enable more accurate and up to date collections.

Other means of keeping records of bibliographic details

Other options for managing references are given below. The time necessary for typing the references with the correct punctuation can be considerable and there is always the likelihood of error. It also takes time to compile the list of references, and any changes to the citations in the text have to be dealt with manually.

Word-processing packages

References can be added into a word processing file using the method of saving the references as a text file as above. The references will probably need to be edited to create the correct style. The user should be assiduous when managing the stored information. Options include creating a new text document for each new library of references or retaining a master document of all references which can then be searched using the usual search/ find function of the software in use. If the references are stored in a table format, the software may have a function to allow them to be sorted into alphabetical or numerical order.

Databases

It is possible to build a personal bibliographic database using commercially available database software. The complexity and functionality of such an imitation off-the-shelf bibliographic reference management file relies on the user's time and competence. A simple solution would be to create a database using basic fields (author, title, date and so on) and then to create a bibliography or list of references using the report function of the database. The researcher would have to balance the time and effort of creating a personal version against any cost of purchasing a commercial package.

Cards and files

It is possible to build a reference library using a printed or written card index or file. Hand writing such entries is time consuming and negates the ability to cut and paste the details into the final document. It can, however, be convenient when working away from one's desk.

Key points

- Be assiduous in keeping records of searches, the relevant records retrieved and of any works accessed
- Save searches for reference and later updating
- Use reference management software if available and if the work warrants it

---

15

INTELLECTUAL PROPERTY AND PLAGIARISM

Chapter outline

- Introduction
- Intellectual property (IP)
- IP considerations when researching and creating documents
- The IP of the researcher's work
- Plagiarism

Introduction

The law regarding intellectual property is likely to affect anyone who is considering using other's work to influence their own work or who wishes to reproduce text, images or other creations whether in hard copy or electronically. The researcher should therefore be aware of how they may be affected so that they can a) remain within the law and b) not commit academic malpractice, even unwittingly. Ignorance is no defence in this area. Conversely, the researcher (or their institution) may be entitled to obtain rights for their work.

Intellectual property (IP)

Intellectual property (IP) law exists in order to protect ideas and creative work from misuse and to allow the creator to gain rewards from their innovations and work. Intellectual property comprises four parts, one of which is copyright. Copyright is likely to be the area that affects the researcher most frequently. The four parts are:

• Copyright
• Patents
• Trade marks
• Designs

The law differs from country to country, although the EU is attempting to standardize regulations within its jurisdiction. There have been moves towards international agreements by WIPO (World Intellectual Property Organization) which is promoting the protection of intellectual property rights in a global context for its member states. In the UK it is the Patent Office which is responsible for IP. The UK statute concerned with this area over recent years has been the Copyright, Designs and Patents Act, 1988, although changes were made on 31 October 2003 to comply with European Directive 2001/29/EC.

Copyright

Copyright protection does not have to be applied for in the same way as other IP rights. It comes into effect automatically and immediately the work is created in a physical form: on paper, on film and so on. It is the work that is protected, not the idea behind that work. The medium of the work may be physical or electronic: all media are protected by copyright.

The Patent Office lists the types of works that copyright protects as:

• original literary works, for example, novels, instruction manuals, computer programs, lyrics for songs, articles in newspapers, some types of databases, but not names or titles (see Trade Marks pages);

- original dramatic works, including works of dance or mime;
- original musical works;
- original artistic works, for example, paintings, engravings, photographs, sculptures, collages, works of architecture, technical drawings, diagrams, maps, logos;
- published editions of works, that is, the typographical arrangement of a publication;
- sound recordings, which may be recordings on any medium, for example, tape or compact disc, and may be recordings of other copyright works, such as musical or literary works;
- films, including videos; and
- broadcasts

(UK Patent Office 2003a)

It should be noted that copyright covers works available on the Internet. A common misconception is that because a work is freely available via the Internet, it is available to be downloaded and used in any way the user wishes. This is not necessarily the case, and researchers should take care with such material to acknowledge and reference sources, gaining permissions where necessary.

It is likely that in the course of information seeking and discovery, a researcher will wish to photocopy works or extracts from works. There are usually guidelines posted near photocopying machines that give details of what may or may not be copied. Researchers should note that photocopies they obtain via document delivery services are for personal use unless they have paid an extra copyright clearance fee.

The Copyright Licensing Agency (CLA) deals in licenses for bodies such as academic institutions and the public service sector. Such licences are designed to enable copying that respects both the needs of creators and publishers, and those of the users. Some works are excluded from licences arranged with the CLA, for example, 'maps,' 'printed music' and 'all UK newspapers' (CLA 2003). Copying under the fair dealing agreement allows additional copying under specified conditions, although this may change, and those wishing to copy should always check that what they intend complies with any licences and the law.

The photocopying bug can be addictive and researchers may find themselves copying anything that is vaguely relevant in case it may be useful. This, of course, costs money and the act of copying does not mean that the information will be learnt by a process of osmosis. Depending on the circumstances and the time available, it can be more beneficial to resort to the practice of note-taking or writing a précis. This can ensure that the researcher understands the work. Care must be taken to retain all reference information.

Libraries will probably answer copyright queries concerning the deposition of materials in an institutional repository. Many publishers allow works, both pre-prints and post-prints, to be deposited in this way.

A copyright balancing act

The balance between providing access to information and protecting the rights of creators is a difficult one which is constantly under discussion. The two opposing sides are the information creators and publishers who wish to benefit financially from their property (except in the case of scholarly works where authors publish to add their work to the research corpus, not for financial gain), and information users who would like information to be freely available. Piracy and commercial misuse hampers industry and further development, but use for educational and private use is often acceptable within limits. Difficulties have been encountered when attempting to agree what is fair use and what may be used without payment or permission. If in any doubt, anyone wishing to use copyright information should contact the rights holder for permission.

Changes in copyright law

There has been much discussion regarding Directive 2001/29/EC of the European Parliament and of the Council of 22 May 2001 on the harmonization of certain aspects of copyright and related rights in the information society. This directive was supposed to have been implemented by member states by December 2002, but in many countries this has not been the case. Fair dealing is one of the areas causing contention in the new directive. One change that users may have noticed is that of the period of time in which a work remains in copyright which has been extended in the UK from 50 to 70 years in order to comply with the EU. This has caused some confusion, as works which had at one stage been out of copyright for some time, were then protected again. Researchers should be able to find advice regarding copyright from libraries, the Patent Office[1] and the UK Government IP information service[2].

Researchers should make sure that they comply with current copyright law when copying, downloading and using materials.

Patents

If an invention can fulfil the criteria of being new, involving an inventive step, is capable of industrial application and is not excluded from certain defined categories, the inventor may apply for, and be granted, a patent. This can then be used to protect their invention from being made, used or sold without the permission of the inventor for a set period of time. UK patents are only applicable within the UK. It is possible to obtain European or international patents for more extensive coverage. Those working in industrial or academic research may wish to apply for patents for their inventions. Full details for the UK may be obtained from the Patent Office.

Trade marks

The Patent Office describes a trade mark as 'any sign which can distinguish the goods and services of one trader from those of another. A sign includes, for example, words, logos, pictures, or a combination of these' (UK Patent Office 2003b). They are used for easy recognition by the general public or others. Domain names for Web sites may also be registered. Unauthorized use of these devices can be a prosecutable offence.

If a researcher is considering developing a trade mark, they should seek advice on registration and other issues. Information is available from the Patent Office.

European Community trademark information can be obtained from the Office for Harmonization of the Internal Market Web site[3].

Designs

The Patent Office in the UK is the body that registers designs resulting in 'a monopoly right for the appearance of the whole or a part of a product resulting from the features of, in particular, the:

- lines
- contours
- colours
- shape
- texture
- materials

of the product or its ornamentation' (Patent Office 2003c).

IP considerations when researching and creating documents

What is allowed?

For many, use of text will amount to the quotation or inclusion of short extracts or ideas which may be acknowledged in the references. If use of materials is not permitted by the rights holders, it is usually made abundantly clear on the item. Where it is not clear if permission is required, it is safest to err on the side of caution and contact the rights holders.

Obtaining permissions

Obtaining permissions can be a time-consuming process and allowances for this should be planned.

It is important to remember that the rights holder and the author/creator may be different. This is often the case with images. If wishing to use any part or excerpt from a publication, check the acknowledgements which should give details of any permissions granted, so that the correct person is contacted in the first instance.

There are some items that are covered by collective management organization. These groups act on behalf of the rights owners by licensing copyright material where it is impractical for the rights owners to act as individuals. Such bodies include the MCPS (Mechanical Copyright Protection Society for the recording of music in any format), the PRS (Performing Rights Society for the public performance and broadcast of musical works) and the CLA (Copyright Licensing Agency) (for the reprographic reproduction of works, that is, photocopying).

Sometimes it is not possible to contact rights holders and where this is the case one sometimes finds words to the effect that every attempt to contact rights holders has been made and the authors would welcome any communication from those who could not be contacted.

The IP of the researcher's work

As stated above, copyright is automatically assigned to the physical manifestation of the researcher's work. This can be emphasized by marking the work with the copyright symbol (©), although this is not strictly necessary.

When submitting articles, papers, book manuscripts and so on, the author should read any rights agreements carefully as they vary from publisher to publisher. Some publishers allow authors to retain the copyright of their work but sign over other publishing rights; others require that the copyright of the work is signed over to the publisher; some may, for example, retain any publishing rights for a set period of time, after which all rights will revert back to the author.

As well as the property rights included in copyright law, the author has certain moral rights. Some statement to this effect often appears on the verso of the title page of a book. An author's moral rights are:

- the right to be identified as the author
- the right to object to their name being associated with some-one else's work
- the right not to have their work subjected to derogatory treatment

Authors are able to take legal proceedings if any of these rights are infringed.

The copyright of a thesis usually belongs to the author, but for a researcher employed by an institution or where there are other agreements, the institution may hold the copyright. Doctoral students and other researchers may find that any intellectual property included in their work is owned by their institution. This should be clarified before taking steps to use the information for any other purpose apart from their research.

As digital encryption and watermarking techniques improve and become more commonplace, authors and publishers of electronic materials may choose to incorporate these features into electronic publications and other electronic sources such as audio visual materials. Watermarking does not necessarily have the effect of preventing unlawful copying, but can authenticate a copy as being a legal copy or include information such as the rights holders' details. This will improve the security of the work as being that of the stated author (rather than someone else who claims it is their own) and can help prevent unlawful copying and misuse.

If it is appropriate, the researcher or their organization may choose to apply for a patent and/or register a design or trade mark. Advice may be required from their institution, the Patent Office or they may need to approach a third party such as a pa-tent agent.

Creative Commons

The Creative Commons is devoted to providing a mechanism for the fair use of works. It has produced a set of freely available copyright licences. The corporation works 'to offer creators a best-of-both-worlds way to protect their works while encouraging certain uses of them' (Creative Commons 2004). A branch of the corporation, International Commons, is dedicated to jurisdictions other than the US. Usage of the Creative Commons licences is growing, and with the addition of more countries, is set to become a standard method of dealing with copyright at an international level.

Plagiarism

Academic institutions and others take plagiarism seriously and it is a subject that researchers and authors should take the trouble to be both aware of and avoid.

What is plagiarism?

Plagiarism can be defined as 'passing off someone else's work, intentionally or unintentionally, as your own, for your own benefit' (Carroll 2002), although there are differences in opinion and confusion in what constitutes plagiarism. It is, however, important to acknowledge all sources used.

One of the keywords in the above definition is 'unintentionally'. This is where the researcher must be particularly alert and sensitive to possible occurrences of plagiarism when composing and checking their own work. Plagiarism can include:

1   'copying a paragraph verbatim from a source without any acknowledgement
2   copying a paragraph and making small changes – e.g. replacing a few verbs, replacing an adjective with a synonym; acknowledgement in the bibliography
3   cutting and pasting a paragraph by using sentences of the

original but omitting one or two and putting one or two in a different order, no quotation marks; with an in-text acknowledgement + bibliography'

(Carroll 2003)

Not only can plagiarism include the actual words written by an author, but also their ideas. A researcher should be careful to acknowledge anything they produce that uses work previously carried out by another, whether the words, the ideas behind the arguments, diagrams or any other work.

All sources should be correctly cited and referenced (see Chapter 13). The researcher should keep impeccable records of their sources of information so that they can check that nothing has been plagiarized and have full details of their sources to include in the list of references.

Software is being developed to aid detection of plagiarized material and a sure way of losing (at the very least) respect in academic circles is to use other's material without acknowledgement. However, most researchers do not need reminding that it is good practice and courteous to acknowledge the work of others.

Tips to help avoid plagiarism

Some useful tips to help avoid plagiarism (as shown in the *Researcher's Companion*[4]) might be to:

* copy direct quotes verbatim to ensure they have not been altered in any way
* be clear when note-taking to include details of the author and source
* become familiar with methods of citing within the text
* only include passages vital to the argument
* record one's own views and thoughts before beginning to find information, then use work by others to support or counter these arguments
* be selective and not include too many quotations
* be careful when paraphrasing that the material is used properly
* write notes from memory after reading the source

Sanctions

Any sanctions resulting from plagiarism will depend upon the circumstances. In more minor cases, a warning may be given or, for academic work, marks may be deducted or an award withheld. For more serious cases, there may be legal implications.

For most, it is a case of educating authors before they fall foul of plagiarism and do not commit it unwittingly.

Key points

- Check the rights associated with any works being used
- Check the rights associated with any work being created
- Be aware of what constitutes plagiarism
- Become familiar with methods that help avoid plagiarism
- Acknowledge all sources

16

THE RESEARCH COMMUNITY AND KEEPING UP TO DATE

Chapter outline

- Introduction
- The research community
- Conferences, conventions and symposia
- Alerting or current awareness services
- Mailing/discussion lists

Introduction

Research can be a lonely pursuit: many hours spent working in a lab or office; reading and writing papers and reports in a highly specialist field with scholars scattered around the world. Conversely, the research community is a global and vibrant hive of activity, which a researcher can tap into easily using electronic communication. In such a fast-moving world, it is vital to keep up to date with the latest developments and monitor work in similar settings. Many researchers thrive on contact with like-minded individuals. Achievements by others can become the inspiration for setting out along new and innovative pathways.

Keeping up to date partly means reading the latest issues of appropriate journals. However, there is a lot more that can be done and an active researcher will spend time mining for the most current and often, unpublished materials. This chapter offers some suggestions for making contact with the research community and keeping abreast of developments.

The research community

Communication between researchers is vital for the dissemination of ideas and results. It is necessary to gather information and communicate with people in both the virtual and real worlds. The community comprises individuals, small groups and large organizations which come together at certain points and in a variety of groupings. See Figure 16.1 for a diagrammatic representation of the research community.

Other institutions

A simple means of finding out about current activities is to access an institution's or research group's Web site. This may or may not include publications and reports of recent activities, but it can be a good starting point and can help identify the individuals or groups involved. They can be found via the HERO Web site or by talking to others working in the same field.

Networking

Leaving a conference clutching a handful of business cards is a common occurrence. Having made the contacts it can be beneficial to keep records of who has been met, where they work and the area in which they are involved before either losing the card or forgetting the detail. Building up a documented network can make the task of locating a person or a place where a specific topic is being researched that much easier. A simple database, spreadsheet or notebook can suffice.

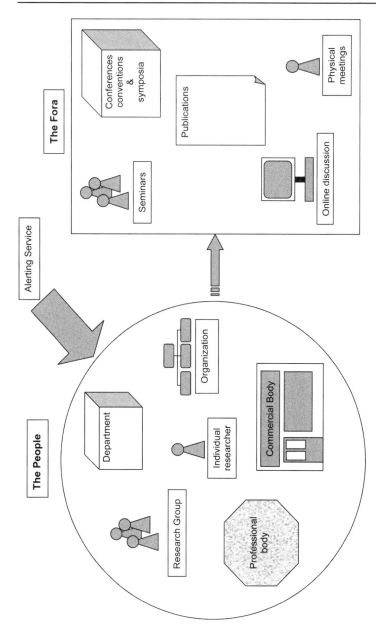

Figure 16.1 The research community

Many researchers become involved in the process of peer review for books or articles. This can be a valuable method of reading items of current interest.

COS and CORDIS

COS and CORDIS are fora for finding details of other researchers and research partners for projects (see Chapter 4).

SOSIG Grapevine and other hubs

The RDN hub, SOSIG[1] (Social Sciences Information Gateway) has developed a networking area of its Web site which has been given the name, SOSIG Grapevine. It is designed to allow users to publicize and find details of conferences and events as well as the opportunity to post and find personal CVs and details of others working in similar subject areas.

The other RDN hubs in the UK provide current awareness services such as those on EEVL for mathematics, computing and engineering.

ISI Highly Cited

ISI Highly Cited forms part of the *ISI Web of Knowledge* service. It provides details of the most cited researchers (those included on the ISI citation databases) and is aiming to extend to the 250 most cited individuals in 21 broad subject categories in the areas of science, engineering and social sciences. The information available includes biographical information and details of publications.

Scenta

Scenta[2] is a portal for the science, engineering and technology (SET) community. It provides the opportunity for users to find out about events and a discussion forum as well as links to resources.

Times Higher Education Supplement

The *Times Higher Education Supplement*[3] (THES) provides information about research funding opportunities (for online subscribers only) and conferences as well as news articles about higher education policy, individuals and current debate. It is available in print and online.

Conferences, conventions and symposia

For the sake of ease, these headings will be referred to under the umbrella term 'conferences.' Gatherings of like-minded researchers are where researchers can discuss (and argue) current research activities with those directly involved. There are conferences in all subject areas. The difficulty can be in knowing about the conferences of offer. Many large conferences are planned many months, or even years in advance. Anyone wishing to submit a paper has to work towards a deadline well ahead of the actual conference. Finding out what is happening on the conference circuit is an important aspect of a researcher's and organization's work. Conference discovery may take place by:

- reading journals
- being a member or obtaining details from a professional body
- accessing subject gateways
- SOSIG Grapevine (see above)
- using a conferences dedicated Web site or directory
- a general Web search
- Web alerts or Weblogs
- mailing/discussion lists
- talking to a colleague or other subject specialist
- print flyers

Conference directories

Many directories are Web based and depend on the conference organizer submitting details to the site. Examples of Web-based multidisciplinary directories are *AllConferences.com*[4] or *Conference Alerts*[5]. Professional societies provide conference information both for their own institute and sometimes for external bodies. For example, the IEEE Ultrasonics, Ferroelectrics, and Frequency Control Society provides access to details of all IEEE conferences, and the Royal Historical Society lists conferences other than its own on its Web pages. Directory based search engines such as *Yahoo!* or the *Google* directory often include a conferences heading under individual subjects.

COS

Registered users of the COS can access its Meetings and Conferences pages which contain information on conferences and meetings as well as calls for papers.

Alerting or current awareness services

So far, this chapter has been about gathering information about the research community and its current activities using action on the part of the researcher. There are many services that enable the researcher to set up sophisticated alerts so that information about publications, events and other matters are automatically delivered to them electronically. These services are often referred to as current awareness or alerting services.

Databases

Most of the subscription online databases provide a facility to save one's searches (see Chapter 6). The user can open up a saved search on entering the database at a later time, to re-run and update it. This is often extended to being able to set up search alerts whereby the search will be automatically re-run at intervals and the user informed of any updates. For example, *Business Source Premier* or *LexisNexis* have this facility. The Elsevier *Science Direct* database provides an additional journal issue alert facility that notifies the user when a new issue of a selected journal becomes available on *Science Direct*. This database also allows the setting up of citation alerts (see Chapter 8). Alert settings can be flexible, allowing the user to select frequency and format of delivery.

Publishers

Traditionally publishers have sent out their catalogues to interested parties to alert them to available publications and tempt them into purchasing copies. This practice is still flourishing but has disadvantages including the cost of the paper, printing and postage, the cost of duplication with outdated mailing lists and irrelevancy because of the recipients being selected by the publisher. An electronic version can be more cost effective and easily managed. In addition, delivery and receipt of the information can be almost instantaneous.

Many of the major publishers such as Blackwells and the Open University Press[6] offer e-mail alerting services for information about new publications. The user is able to specify the subject area(s) of interest.

The BSI Group (British Standards) has an e-mail news service providing information about developments and other items of interest for subscribers.

Official publications

For official publications in the UK, the Stationery Office (TSO) newsletter provides an alerting service. The TSO is historically the publisher to government and Parliament but has extended to offering information management solutions. It has an alerting service whereby the user can request to receive information about recent TSO, regulatory and official publications, on topics selected by the user.

Tables of contents (TOC) services

Tables of contents alerts are particularly useful as the user is made aware of all the items within a particular publication. This means that, although they will be alerted to some articles which are of no interest, there may be items about related subjects that would not have been selected by a keyword search.

ZETOC

For those eligible to use *Zetoc*, alerts can be set up to inform the user of tables of contents of publications as they are added to the vast collection of the British Library's Tables of Contents of journals and conference proceedings. The user may set up multiple alerts using one or more titles and the results are delivered by e-mail.

Databases such as those provided by CSA can be set up for TOC alerting. This can be achieved by running a search using one or more sources (using a journal title or ISSN) then saving the search as an alert. New additions to the results will then be sent automatically to the subscriber.

Journal publishers such as Sage[7], OUP[8] and Springer[9] provide a table of contents alerting service. The recipient may receive information about forthcoming articles and papers in advance of publication. The Springer Keyword alerts service allows the user to submit keywords as the basis for an altering service.

SARA (Scholarly Articles Research Alerting) delivers tables of contents of journals from a number of publishers to anyone who requests them (SARA 2004). Users select subject categories and are sent details of contents prior to publication.

Commercial document supply services such as InfoTrieve[10] sometimes offer a table of contents alerting service to which the user can subscribe by setting up their own profile.

Research news

Research news is made available via a number of sources: professional bodies, charities and academic departments. Some examples include the National Society for Epilepsy and the University of Newcastle upon Tyne's *Newslink*.

Other fora such as *EurekAlert* from the American Association for the Advancement of Science[11] (AAAS) enable researchers to post news about their work which can then be accessed by others. These initiatives demand submission of items by researchers or their institutions.

Web alerts

Some search engines provide a means of saving searches for later re-running. The user might have to initiate the search each time; it will not necessarily be run automatically. For example, the *Yahoo* search engine has this feature in its *My Yahoo* section. Although a search engine feature affected by the drawbacks of using the WWW, it can be a useful means of re-running useful searches and updating information.

Mailing/discussion lists

Mailing lists are a means of monitoring current topics of interest and taking part in discussion with others working in a similar field. There is a danger in joining too many lists and becoming inundated with e-mails. There are lists in most disciplines, varying from the general to the highly specific. The activity of the lists varies from those where subscribers may receive many messages each day to those which lie dormant for long periods. Surveying the archives gives the user a feel for the amount of activity on any list. Fortunately, there are means by which a user's subscription can be suspended during times of inactivity such as during vacations, so that on return there are not hundreds of new e-mails waiting.

Although many lists are open to all, some are closed, that is, available only to those complying with specific criteria (for example, those for Heads of Departments). Lists are monitored by a list manager who steps in if the service is being abused or if irrelevant or contentious messages are being sent.

In UK higher and further education circles there are many lists sponsored by the JISC in the Jiscmail[12] national academic mailing list service. There is no cost to the list subscriber or the list manager for these lists. Globally there are numerous lists in existence that run using the commercial LISTSERV[13] software. It is possible to search for lists that use this system using the company's own Catalist search engine service.

The UK Office of Science and Technology has developed the *Researchers Forum*[14] to promote online discussion between researchers in academia, commerce and other institutions. The archives are available for all, but any person wishing to post messages must first register.

Key points

- Find ways of contacting and monitoring other researchers, research groups and institutions
- Keep up with conference activity in the selected subject area
- Set up alerts to stay informed of new publications
- Join a mailing list to monitor current developments and to contact those working in similar subjects

---

17

THE CHANGING LANDSCAPE OF RESEARCH

Chapter outline

- Introduction
- JISC activities
- Open access
- Searching for research materials
- Open URLs
- e-books and e-theses
- The e-science programme and the Grid
- Means of managing and presenting information
- Digital preservation and curation
- Research Libraries Network
- Journal impact factors and citation indexes

Introduction

The combination of improving research support in libraries, increasing numbers of researchers, the importance of the RAE (Research Assessment Exercise) in UK universities and the drive towards enhanced scholarly communication, all married with technological developments, result in fast-moving developments in research information provision, storage and access.

JISC activities

The JISC national Information Environment (IE) 'is the set of networked services that allows people to discover, access, use and publish' (Powell and Lyon 2002) scholarly materials via secure and seamless channels. It (and its technical architecture) addresses problems such as multiple interfaces and the large numbers of resources available. The IE programme comprises a number of strands, the main ones being:

1. development of online portals for searching concurrently across multiple resources
2. encouraging collaboration between members of the education community to develop, submit and share electronic resources
3. development of a means of storing and manipulating information using portals so that users may 'interact with relevant resources according to subject, institutional and personal profiles' (JISC 2004c)
4. investigation of issues associated with using information resources whilst also using VLEs (Virtual Learning Environments)

Four JISC *Join-up* projects[1] are investigating seamless links between resource discovery and access of journal articles. They cover the areas of cross-searching multiple databases using a single user-friendly portal or interface, location of the most appropriate copy by bridging the gap between resource discovery and access, integrated document delivery and enhancement of the ZETOC service.

Open access

Open access is making materials, for example, research findings and papers, freely available to the research community. It is a means of publishing and sharing research findings. Stephen Harnad has described the scenario of freely available materials, with interlinked citations, links to previous and subsequent versions and reviews together with new impact indicators as 'inevitable' (Harnad 2001). As the research landscape moves closer towards this model, researchers will have greater access to more materials, at an increased rate of exchange and with greater interaction (see Chapter 11).

This situation is being fuelled by academic institutions unhappy with the current journal subscription model which includes barriers to access such as rapid rates of increase in cost. The move towards alternative sources of, if not free, at least affordable resources, is gathering pace.

Coupled with that, there is much unrest regarding the traditional subscription/site licence/pay-per-view publishing stranglehold (Harnad 2001) and libraries may not be able to afford certain subscriptions. This situation is all the more confusing, as the originator of the material was probably not seeking financial reward for the publication of the work, but the library has to pay for access to it.

As the tensions between journal publishers, libraries and scholarly authors continue, the mode of dissemination of research output could change markedly from its traditional journal-based format to a less validated, but more accessible version.

Concern about the lack of prestige of open access journals is waning as increasing numbers of respected titles and publishers offer this mode of publication. Also, items are being peer-reviewed and impact factors for open access titles are being calculated which serve to engender confidence in them.

Open access journals are creating new models for funding the publishing process that result in free access for the end user and possibly increased citations (that is, impact) for the author. It must be clarified that open access information published in respected journals often requires the author (or their institution) to pay to cover publishing costs. This model is used, for example, in the *Company of Biologists* journals[2] (*Development, Journal of Cell Science* and *The Journal of Experimental Biology*). Publishers such as this are responding to pressure for an alternative to subscription payment for research literature.

Having research materials, including the original data, freely available online allows the researcher to follow the history (and accuracy) of items and track back from an article to the original data upon which it was based. Such information can be used to support the 'accuracy, currency and validity' of work (Lyon 2003). This issue of provenance is being investigated as part of the eBank UK project[3].

The SPARC initiative

SPARC (the Scholarly Publishing and Academic Resources Coalition) aims to address some of the problems associated with current modes of disseminating scholarly information. The coalition comprises universities, research libraries and other organizations (and has a partner in Europe, SPARC Europe[4]).

The publishing partners have been drawn from the scientific, technical and medical (STM) community, although this is changing to include the humanities and social sciences. SPARC has three main objectives:

- encouragement of alternative, but respected, vehicles for publication to provide competition to high-cost journals
- acting as an advocate for change and the means by which it is achieved through communication, outreach and public relations activities
- raising awareness of scholarly communication issues (SPARC 2003)

There are approximately two dozen or so publishing partners, about one third of which offer open access, that is, without charging subscriptions. All SPARC endorsed journals are available in electronic format and some publish an accompanying print version. SPARC supports the Open Archives Initiative (see Chapter 11).

Searching for research materials

Cross-searching

Cross-searching is searching across a number of sites in a single action using a specially developed interface. This is convenient for the searcher, but technically causes some difficulties. The searcher benefits from saving time and effort by not having to search a multiplicity of databases with an equal number of interfaces. Cross-searching is also a means of the user discovering resource providers of which they may have been previously unaware. Libraries are beginning to provide such facilities so that users may search other databases from the same interfaces as their catalogues. An additional issue is that of the user discovering the most appropriate source of information. Cross-searching forms an element of the JISC IE infrastructure programme.

Semantic Web

The semantic Web (and subsequently, the semantic grid) is a method of giving meaning to data accessible on the Web. Work is taking place on the development of ontologies, or the creation of shared, common vocabularies. The reason for this is (partly) to enable more effective discovery of information on the Web. It works by computers becoming 'much better able to process and "understand" the data that they merely display at present' (Berners-Lee, Hendler and Lassila 2001: 2). If computers accurately ascertain and manipulate the semantics of the description of content, then information retrieval should result in more relevant information than the current process.

Text mining

Text mining is a technique for 'the intelligent retrieval of textual information against complex search criteria' (JISC 2003b). This development is of interest in the research community for aiding the retrieval of relevant information from an ever-growing corpus of literature and data.

Open URLs

The development of the Open URL framework will allow a Web based scholarly service to link to the most appropriate copy of extended resources. The extended resources might be links:

- 'from a citation in a journal article to a record in a library catalogue that shows the library holdings of the cited journal;
- from a journal title to impact factor information in ISI's Journal Citation Reports;
- from a stock ticker symbol found in a record from the ABI/ Inform database to on-line stock information;
- from title words or subject headings of a scholarly article to related information in Internet search engines' (Van de Sompel and Beit-Arie 2001)

The emphasis is on the user (which may the library) requesting the links, and allows links to be added which are context sensitive in a particular location. For example, a librarian may link directly from a citation to a full text electronic journal or to the library catalogue which gives details of print holdings, depending on the situation. Many information providers (for example, Ebsco, the Gale Group and Cambridge Scientific Abstracts) include Open URLs in their resources. The benefits for researchers are many and the use of Open URLs will contribute to seamless linking and improved resource discovery in the information environment.

e-books and e-theses

e-books

e-books have had a mixed inception and reception. There have been a variety of methods of delivery and viewing, and payment and protection models: PC based systems are gaining popularity over hand-held devices. There are benefits of having a digital book such as the search capabilities, the concept of micro-purchase (that is, the purchase of a small section of a publication say, a page at a time) and the possibility of linking to other multimedia sources.

There are still many unanswered questions and nervousness on the part of publishers, providers and purchasers/mediators. The electronic format is probably here to stay, but how it is manifested will take promotion, negotiation and time. And the future of the printed book seems assured, certainly for the foreseeable future.

e-theses and dissertations

As mentioned previously, the UK has been slow to develop a national initiative for the provision of electronic theses and dissertations. Work is underway to improve this situation by:

a) provision of national recommendations for creating, storing, organizing, managing and accessing electronic theses[5]
b) development of an ETD submission system for use in the UK
c) inclusion of theses as part of open archive collections[6]
d) the opportunities and potential of born digital theses for the UK
e) creation of a national ETD resource holding base

This area of provision will be developing rapidly in the future.

The e-science programme and the Grid

Researchers have always drawn on the work of others. The development of the e-science programme and the Grid is the catalyst for a leap forward in collaboration and use of data for research on a global scale. It will also provide access to the experimental facilities and computing capability that enable this collaboration. As the Director General of the Research Councils, John Taylor stated, 'e-science is about global collaboration in key areas of science, and the next generation of infrastructure that will enable it' (UK Research Councils 2002).

The core of the e-science programme involves the creation of a means of 'sharing of computing resources, data resources and experimental facilities' (Hey and Trefethen 2003: 2) for vast amounts of data. Although sharing resources began in science, there are plans to develop a similar facility for the arts and humanities. Also, application of grid technology within e-social science is being developed such as the projects being funded by the ESRC.

'Grid computing is applying the resources of many computers in a network to a single problem at the same time' (Berman, Fox and Hey 2003) and is the underlying technical architecture that supports the e-science programme. As well as sharing computing power, it will enable users to share databases and other tools. It has been explained on the e-science Web site by differentiating it from the WWW:

> The Grid supports complete process initiation and execution including any necessary data location and retrieval. You will ask questions and not know what computer was used to process the data, or where the data came from. This allows it to carry out significantly large tasks and opens up new capabilities for knowledge generation.
>
> (e-science 2004)

Collaborative e-research

The Grid will be one means of supporting collaborative e-research. As data gathering increases to almost unimaginable levels and more research is developed in new areas such as interdisciplinary subjects (for example, bioinformatics), the resulting 'data deluge' will need to be managed and maintained (Hey and Trefethen 2003). The benefits of scale of a number of centres working collaboratively will contribute to the success of such developments. Collaborative e-research will form a part of any future global virtual research environment.

Means of managing and presenting information

Increasingly institutions are employing the use of systems such as VLEs, managed learning environments (MLEs) and portals as teaching and learning vehicles and for managing and presenting information. The researcher may encounter one or more of these systems (although not strictly designed specifically for the research community) which usually require some form of authentication such as a password. Usage and terminology varies widely and terms are often used interchangeably. The following provides a simplified explanation of these systems.

VLE

A VLE is a system that enables online communication between learners and tutors for the purpose of learning. There may be facilities such as discussion fora, links to resources, a means of tracking student activity on the VLE, and the ability to create, display and complete quizzes. A VLE can form a part of an MLE (see below).

MLE

An MLE may comprise many different systems that aid the management of learning & teaching, administrative records and data. It may include a VLE as a sub-system.

Portal

Portals are often confused with Gateways (see Chapter 10).

Digital preservation and curation

A major concern of those working in information is that of long-term preservation and curation of digital materials. Either the storage of information has to change to match the access facilities, or the method of storage has to be able to be accessed by whatever means available, perhaps by creating a means of emulating the original hardware or software, however long a period has elapsed since the materials were archived (Granger 2000). An example of a problem of digital materials being created and stored in the past, which became inaccessible is the BBC's Domesday project. This took place in 1986 and the data was stored on the now superseded LV-ROM videodisc (Abbott 2003). Researchers have finally solved this particular problem with work carried out at the Universities of Leeds (UK) and Michigan (USA).

In the UK a body has been set up called the Digital Preservation Coalition (DPC) 'to foster joint action to address the urgent challenges of securing the preservation of digital resources in the UK and to work with others internationally to secure our global digital memory and knowledge base' (DPC 2003). Members of the DPC include institutions such as the British Library, the e-science Core Programme and the University of London Computer Centre.

A national centre has been set up 'to lead research and development into key areas of digital curation for data and publications, and to pilot the development of generic support services for maintaining digital data and research results over their entire life-cycle for current and future users.' This Digital Curation Centre[7] is investigating how vast amounts of trusted electronic data (publications and other resources) can be archived, preserved and managed in the long-term for future users.

Research Libraries Network (RLN)

One of the recommendations of the investigations by the Research Support Libraries Group (RSLG 2003) was the creation of a national network of research support provided by research libraries in the UK. This network will be lead and co-ordinated by a new body, the Research Libraries Network, which will have three roles:

- providing strategic leadership for the provision of research information in the UK

- ensuring the RLN programme is funded and implemented
- acting as an advocate for research information

This national approach will change the landscape of research information provision in the UK, although there are many issues yet to be resolved before any solutions are selected, shaped and put into place.

Journal impact factors and citation indexes

Academics have been familiar with journal impact factors for some time. This is a means of scoring journals using ratings and is used by authors to aid selection of journals for publication. Impact factors are also used during the RAE process where they have a bearing on the outcomes. The current crude method of measurement is being challenged by, for example, the developing BioMed model which will attempt to assess 'the value of individual articles using a combination of editorial and peer judgements,' (BioMed Central 2004) in addition to the more common citation rates and usage statistics.

There are a number of issues associated with the current practice of compiling citation indexes. Work is beginning to create a more reliable and wider index for open access journals. An international working group may be created to investigate the problems and possible solutions for a citation index for open access journals.

GLOSSARY

Abstract	A summary of an article.
Appropriate copy	The version of an item which is most appropriate to the context of the user.
Athens	An authentication service used to validate the eligibility of the user to access a resource. Many information providers allow Athens authentication.
Boolean operators	(or connectors) a means of using the principle of logic devised by a nineteenth-century mathematician: AND, OR and NOT.
Call number	A number assigned to each item so that it may be retrieved (see also classification number and shelfmark).
Catalogue	A list of all the library's holdings. May be printed or available online.
Catalogue record	The information about a work stored on a catalogue.
Classification system	A means of organizing items by subject, keeping like subjects together.
Classification number	A number assigned to each item, determined by a classification schedule and enabling orderly shelving and retrieval. See also call number and shelfmark.

Closed access	When items are stored so they are not accessible by users. Items are requested by users and fetched for them by library staff.
Collection	A collective term for the holdings of a library. One library may have many discrete collections.
Concurrent users	The number of people using the same resource at the same time.
Dissertation	A publication forming a requirement for an academic taught course.
Document delivery/supply	The supply of documents from a remote source.
Electronic resource	Any information supplied electronically. Typical resources include e-journals, online databases and CD-ROMs.
Ephemera	Publications such as leaflets or forms which are not formally published and have no bibliographic record at the time of publication.
e-print	A research paper in electronic format. It may be a pre-print (before being refereed) or a post-print (after being refereed). It could, for example, be a journal article, working paper or conference paper.
Freely available	At no monetary cost to the user and with no authentication required.
Grey literature	Publications that are not created and made available via formal means and therefore have no bibliographic record when published. Includes: theses and conference proceedings.
Interlibrary loan	A means of obtaining items not held at the home library.
Item	A single manifestation of a work.
Licence	An agreement between the user (or more commonly the institution) and the supplier of a service (usually an electronic resource). Conditions of use form part of the licence.
Loan entitlement	The numbers of items that a user is permitted to borrow and the length of time for which they may retain those items.

Microform	A format that requires magnification to be able to see the content.
Open access	Items that the library user may access for themselves on open shelves or electronic resources made freely available.
Query	The term(s) used for searching.
Repository	An electronic store of (usually) research output including pre-prints, post-prints, bibliographic information and other materials. May be open access.
Serial	A publication that is issued in successive, numbered (or chronological) parts with no set end date.
Shelfmark	The numbers and/or letters assigned to each item so it may be retrieved. May include other characters as well as the classmark. See also classmark and call number.
Stopword	A word in common usage that a search function will not allow or will ignore as it would produce too many results. For example: the; of; for; that.
Subscription	A fee paid for a service or resource, usually for a designated period of time.
Thesis	A publication resulting from doctoral research and submitted in fulfilment of the award of PhD (or similar).
Work	A manifestation of an author's/creator's output; for example, *War and Peace* by Trollope, or *Pictures at an Exhibition* by Mussorgsky.

REFERENCES AND BIBLIOGRAPHY

Abbott, D. (2003) Overcoming the dangers of technical obsolescence: rescuing the BBC Domesday project. *Digicult.Info*, 4, pp. 7–10. Digicult. August. http://www.digicult.info/pages/newsletter.php (accessed 22 February 2004)

ADT (Australian Digital Theses) (2003) *ADT Homepage*. Council of Australian University Librarians: Canberra. http://adt.caul.edu.au/ (accessed 22 February 2004)

Alkire, Leland G. (ed.) (2003) *Periodical Title Abbreviations*, 14th edn. London: Gale

Allen, R. E. (ed.) (1991) *The Concise Oxford Dictionary*, 8th edn. Oxford: Oxford University Press

Andrew, T. (2003) Trends in self-posting of research material online by academic staff. *Ariadne*, 37, 30 October. UKOLN: Bath. http://www.ariadne.ac.uk/issue37/andrew/ (accessed 22 February 2004)

Armstrong, C. J., Lonsdale, R. E., Stoker, D. A. and Urquhart, C. J. (2000) *Final Report – 1999/2000 Cycle*. JUSTEIS JISC Usage Surveys: Trends in Electronic Information Services August. Department of Information Studies, University of Wales: Aberystwyth. http://www.dil.aber.ac.uk/dils/research/justeis/cyc1rep0.htm (accessed 23 February 2004)

BBSRC (2003) *Multidisciplinary Research: Why Do Research at the Interface?* Swindon: Biotechnology and Biological Sciences Research Council. http://www.bbsrc.ac.uk/science/spotlight/multi.html (accessed 22 February 2004)

Berman, F., Fox, G. and Hey, T. (eds) (2003) *Grid Computing: Making the Global Infrastructure a Reality*. Chichester: John Wiley & Sons Ltd.

Publisher's website. http://www.wileyeurope.com/WileyCDA/ WileyTitle/productCd–0470853190.html (accessed 26 January 2004)

Berners-Lee, T., Hendler, J. and Lassila, O. (2001) The Semantic Web: A new form of Web content that is meaningful to computers will unleash a revolution of new possibilities, *Scientific American*, May. http://www.sciam.com/article.cfm?articleID=00048144–10D2–1C70– 84A9809EC588EF21&pageNumber=1&catID=2 (accessed 22 February 2004)

BioMed Central (2004) *What is BioMed Central?* London: BioMed Central. http://www.biomedcentral.com/info/ (accessed 22 February 2004)

Bradley, P. (2004) *Welcome to Phil Bradley's Home Page.* Phil Bradley http://www.philb.com/ (accessed 1 March 2004)

British Library (2004) *Reader Admissions.* London: The British Library. http://www.bl.uk/services/reading/admissions.html (accessed 21 February 2004)

BSI (British Standards Institution) (1989) BS 1629: 1989. *Recommendations for References to Published Materials*

Buzan, Tony (2002) *How to Mind Map.* London: Thorsons

Carroll, J. (2002) *A Handbook for Deterring Plagiarism in Higher Education.* Oxford: Oxford Brookes University, in W. Johnston (2003) The Concept of Plagiarism, *Learning and Teaching in Action*, **2** (1). Manchester Metropolitan University. http://www.ltu.mmu.ac.uk/ltia/issue4/johnston.shtml (accessed 22 February 2004)

Carroll, J. (2003) *Plagiarism: Is There a Virtual Solution?* (Based on an exercise in Academic Writing for Graduate Students by Swales and Feale, University of Michigan, 1993). Oxford: Oxford Centre for Staff and Learning Development, Oxford Brookes University. http://www. brookes.ac.uk/services/ocsd/2_learntch/plagiarism.html (accessed 22 February 2004)

CAS (2004) *About CAS.* Ohio: Chemical Abstracts Service. http:// www.cas.org/about.html (accessed 22 February 2004)

CLA (Copyright Licensing Agency) (2003) *List of Excluded Categories and Excluded Works.* London: Copyright Licensing Agency. http:// www.cla.co.uk/have_licence/support/excluded.html (accessed 22 February 2004)

Creative Commons (2004) *About Us. 'Some Rights Reserved': Building a Layer of Reasonable Copyright.* Stanford, California: Creative Commons. http://creativecommons.org/learn/aboutus/ (accessed 7 March 2004)

CURL (2003) *CURL Membership and Partnership Guidelines: Guidelines for Membership.* Consortium of University Research Libraries. http:// www.curl.ac.uk/members/guidelines.html (accessed 22 February 2004)

Day, M. (2003) Prospects for institutional e-print repositories in the

United Kingdom. *ePrints UK supporting study, no. 1*. Bath: UKOLN. http://www.rdn.ac.uk/projects/eprints-uk/docs/studies/impact/ (accessed 22 February 2004)

Department of Health (DH) and Her Majesty's Prison Service (2003) *A Pharmacy Service for Prisoners*. London, Department of Health: Prison Health Report. http://www.dh.gov.uk/assetRoot/04/06/57/07/04065 707.pdf (accessed 22 February 2004)

DOAJ (Directory of Open Access Journals) (2003) *About: Definitions*. http://www.doaj.org/articles/about/ (accessed 22 February 2004)

Dobratz, S. and Mattaei, B. (2003) Open archives activities and experiences in Europe: An overview by the Open Archives Forum. *D-Lib Magazine*, **9** (1), January. http://www.dlib.org/dlib/january03/dobratz/01dobratz.html (accessed 22 February 2004)

Dolphin, I., Miller, P. and Sherratt, R. (2002) Portals, portals everywhere, *Ariadne*, 33, 10 October. Bath: UKOLN. http://www.ariadne.ac.uk/issue33/portals/ (accessed 22 February 2004)

DPC (Digital Preservation Coalition) (2003) *Welcome to the Digital Preservation Coalition website*. London: Digital Preservation Coalition. http://www.dpconline.org/graphics/index.html (accessed 22 February 2004)

e-science (2004) *e-Science and Grid Definitions*. Department of Trade and Industry and the UK Research Councils. London: HMSO. http://www.escience-grid.org.uk/docs/gridtech/define.htm (accessed 22 February 2004)

Elmes, Helen (ed.) (2003) *Commonwealth Universities Yearbook*. London: Association of Commonwealth Universities

EU (European Union) (2004) *Official Journal of the European Union*. EU Publications Office. http://publications.eu.int/general/en/oj_en.htm and http://europa.eu.int/eur-lex/en/search/search_oj.html (on Eur-lex) (accessed 23 February 2004)

Expert Information (2004) *Index to Theses*. London: Expert Information, Index to theses http://www.theses.com/ (accessed 22 February 2004)

Feather, John (1999) *Survey of Microform Sets: A Report for Research Support Libraries Programme*. Research Support Libraries Programme (RSLP) http://www.rslp.ac.uk/Studies/Feather.doc (accessed 22 February 2004)

Fisher, D. and Hanstock, T. (2003) *Citing References: A Guide for Users*, 5th edn. Nottingham Trent University: Libraries and learning resources. http://www.ntu.ac.uk/llr/library/citingrefs.htm#oth (accessed 22 February 2004)

Gabriel (2004) *Welcome to Gabriel*. Conference of European National Librarians (CENL) http://portico.bl.uk/gabriel/ (accessed 22 February 2004)

Granger, S. (2000) Emulation as a digital preservation strategy. *D-lib magazine*, **6** (10), October. http://www.dlib.org/dlib/october00/granger/10granger.html (accessed 1 March 2004)

Harnad, S. (2001) For whom the gate tolls? How and why to free the refereed research literature online through author/institution self-archiving, now. *Cogprints*. University of Southampton. http://cogprints.ecs.soton.ac.uk/archive/00001639/index.html (accessed 26 January 2004). Published as: Harnad, S. (2003) Open access to peer-reviewed research through author/institution self-archiving: maximizing research impact by maximizing online access, in D. Law and J. Andrews (eds) (2003) *Digital Libraries: Policy Planning and Practice.* Aldershot: Ashgate Publishing

Hawkins, L. and Hirons, J. (2002) Transforming AACR2: Using the revised rules in Chapters 9 and 12. Workshop presentation at *NASIG (North American Serials Interest Group) 17th Annual Conference. Transforming Serials: The Revolution Continues*, Williamsburg, VA, 20–23 June 2002. http://www.loc.gov/acq/conser/ (accessed 22 February 2004)

Hey, T. and Trefethen, A. (2003) The data deluge: an e-science perspective, in F. Berman, G. Fox and T. Hey (eds) (2003) *Grid Computing: Making the Global Infrastructure a Reality*. Chichester: John Wiley & Sons Ltd. http://www.rcuk.ac.uk/escience/documents/report_datadeluge.pdf (accessed 22 February 2004)

HMSO (2003) *Access to Information*. Her Majesty's Stationery Office. http://www.hmso.gov.uk/information/access_information.htm (accessed 22 February 2004)

Hodgson, Kate (2002) Vulcan crosswords and dodgy deadlines, *Academic News*. London: Sweet & Maxwell. Autumn. https://www.smlawpub.co.uk/academic/acad02.pdf (accessed 22 February 2004)

IALS (Institute of Advanced Legal Studies) (2002) *Current Legal Research Topics Database Project*. Institute of Advanced Legal Studies. London: University of London. http://ials.sas.ac.uk/library/clrt/clrt.htm (accessed 23 February 2004)

IFLA (2003) *Library and Information Science: Citation Guides for Electronic Documents*. The Hague: International Federation of Library Associations and Institutions http://www.ifla.org/I/training/citation/citing.htm (accessed 22 February 2004)

JISC (2003a) *Resource Guide for the Physical Sciences*. Manchester: Joint Information Systems Committee. http://www.jisc.ac.uk/index.cfm?name=rg_physci_access (accessed 26 February 2004). Identical information is given in the JISC resource guides for other subjects.

JISC (2003b) *Circular 7/03: National Centre for Text Mining – Call for Expressions of Interest*. JISC (Joint Information Systems Committee).

http://www.jisc.ac.uk/index.cfm?name=funding_textminingcentre (accessed 26 February 2004)

JISC (2004a) *Portals: Frequently Asked Questions.* JISC (Joint Information Systems Committee). http://www.jisc.ac.uk/index.cfm?name=ie_portalsfaq (accessed 26 February 2004)

JISC (2004b) *Focus on Access to Institutional Resources (FAIR) Programme.* JISC (Joint Information Systems Committee). http://www.jisc.ac.uk/index.cfm?name=programme_fair (accessed 1 March 2004)

JISC (2004c) *Investing in the Future: Developing an Online Information Environment.* JISC (Joint Information Systems Committee). http://www.jisc.ac.uk/index.cfm?name=ie_home (accessed 1 March 2004)

Law Library (2003) *Cardiff Index to Legal Abbreviations.* Cardiff University Information Services. http://www.legalabbrevs.cardiff.ac.uk (accessed 26 February 2004)

Lawrence, S., Giles, C. L. and Bollacker, K. (1999) Digital libraries and autonomous citation indexing, *IEEE Computer*, **32**, 6: 67–71

Legal Deposit Libraries Act (2003) (c. 28). London: HMSO. http://www.legislation.hmso.gov.uk/acts/acts2003/20030028.htm (accessed 23 February 2004)

LSE (London School of Economics) (2004) *The Library.* British Library of Political and Economic Science. London. http://www.lse.ac.uk/library/ (accessed 23 February 2004)

Lynch, C. (2001) The battle to define the future of the book in the digital world, *First Monday*, **6** (6), 4 June. http://www.firstmonday.dk/issues/issue6_6/lynch (accessed 26 February 2004)

Lyon, L. (2003) eBank UK: Building the links between research data, scholarly communication and learning, *Ariadne*, issue 36, July. Bath: UKOLN. http://www.ariadne.ac.uk/issue36/lyon/ (accessed 1 March 2004)

McKiernan, Gerry (2003) *All that JAS: Journal Abbreviation Sources.* Iowa State University. http://www.public.iastate.edu/~CYBERSTACKS/JAS.htm (accessed 23 February 2004)

NDLTD (Networked Digital Library of Theses and Dissertations) (2003) *Objectives of NDLTD.* http://www.ndltd.org/ (accessed 23 February 2004)

Notess, G. (2003) *Why Search Engine Size Matters.* SearchEngineShowdown. http://www.searchengineshowdown.com/stats/sizematters.shtml (accessed 23 February 2004)

ONS (Office for National Statistics) (2004) *Welcome to National Statistics Online.* Office for National Statistics, Newport. http://www.national-statistics.gov.uk/ (accessed 23 February 2004)

Ordnance Survey (2004) *Site Home Page.* Southampton: Ordnance Survey.

http://www.ordnancesurvey.co.uk/oswebsite/ (accessed 23 February 2004)

Orna, E. with Stevens, G. (2000) *Managing Information for Research.* Buckingham: Open University Press

Paskin, N. (2003) DOI: a 2003 progress report. *D-Lib Magazine*, **9** (6), June. http://www.dlib.org/dlib/june03/paskin/06paskin.html (accessed 23 February 2004)

PLoS (Public Library of Science) (2003) *About PLoS: Missions and Goals.* http://www.plos.org/about/index.html (accessed 26 January 2004)

Powell, A. and Lyon, L. (2002) The JISC Information Environment and web services, *Ariadne*, 31, April. Bath: UKOLN. http://www. ariadne.ac.uk/issue31/information-environments/intro.html (accessed 23 February 2004)

Raistrick, D. (1993) Index to legal citations and abbreviations, 2nd edn. London: Bowker-Saur

RCUK (Research Councils UK) (2004) *Welcome.* Swindon: Research Councils UK. http://www.rcuk.ac.uk/ (accessed 23 February 2004)

Reynard, K. W. (ed.) (2002) *Aslib Directory of Information Sources in the United Kingdom*, 12th edn. London: ASLIB

Richards, M. P. (2002) *The Evolution of Hominid Dietary Adaptations Linked with Environmental Changes: Extending the Record beyond 100,000 Years.* NERC Funding Council Research Grant. Available at: http://www. nerc.ac.uk/funding/thematics/efched/abstractsofawards.shtml (accessed 23 February 2004)

RSLG (Research Support Libraries Group) (2003), *Final Report.* London: HEFCE (Higher Education Funding Council for England). http:// www.rslg.ac.uk/final/final.pdf (accessed 23 February 2004)

RSLP (2001) *Invitation to Tender: Scoping Study and Implementation Plan for a Serials Union Catalogue (SUNCAT).* News and Events. Research Support Libraries Programme. http://www.rslp.ac.uk/News/2001/suncat.htm (accessed 23 February 2004)

Rubinstein, Artur (1998) Chopin: Fantaisie-Impromptu in C sharp minor Opus 66, in *Great Pianists of the 20th Century.* [CD recording] Philips Classics 456 955–2, Track 5. Recorded 1964

SARA (2004) *Scholarly Articles Research Alerting.* London: Taylor and Francis. http://www.tandf.co.uk/sara/ (accessed 1 March 2004)

Sharp, J. A., Peters, J. and Howard, K. (2002) *The Management of a Student Research Project*, 3rd edn. Aldershot: Gower.

Shoemaker, Donald (2000) *Theories of Delinquency: An Examination of Explanations of Delinquent Behaviour.* Oxford: Oxford University Press

Simpson, P. (2002) E-Prints and the Open Archive Initiative – Opportunities for Libraries, in J. W. Markham (ed.) *IAMSLIC 2002 Conference*

Proceedings Bridging the Digital Divide. Mazatlan, Sinaloa, Mexico. Oct 6–11. http://tardis.eprints.org/papers/ (accessed 26 January 2004)

SPARC (2003) *About SPARC: What does SPARC do?* Washington, DC: SPARC (Scholarly Publishing and Academic Resources Coalition). http://www.arl.org/sparc (accessed 1 March 2004)

Sullivan, D. (2003) *Search Engine Sizes: Current Size Comparison.* Search Engine Watch http://www.searchenginewatch.com/reports/article.php/2156481 (accessed 23 February 2004)

UK Patent Office (2003a) *Copyright: What is Copyright?* Newport: The Patent Office. http://www.patent.gov.uk/copy/definition.htm (accessed 23 February 2004)

UK Patent Office (2003b) *Trademarks: What is a Trademark?* Newport: The Patent Office. http://www.patent.gov.uk/tm/whatis/definition.htm (accessed 23 February 2004)

UK Patent Office (2003c) *Designs: What is a Design?* Newport: The Patent Office. http://www.patent.gov.uk/design/definition.htm (accessed 23 February 2004)

UK Research Councils (2002) *e-science. First Phase of the Programme.* Swindon: Research Councils UK. http://www.rcuk.ac.uk/escience/archive/phase1.asp (accessed 22 February 2004)

Van de Sompel, H. and Beit-Arie, O. (2001) Open linking in the scholarly information environment using the OpenURL framework, *D-Lib Magazine,* **7** (3). http://www.dlib.org/dlib/march01/vandesompel/03vandesompel.html#fig1 (accessed 23 February 2004)

Vivisimo (2004) *FAQ.* Pittsburg: Vivisimo Inc. http://vivisimo.com/html/faq/Overview.html (accessed 8 March 2004)

Wang, Eryu (1995) *Studies on the Genomes of Wild-type and Vaccine Strains of Yellow Fever Virus.* PhD Thesis, University of Surrey.

Wellcome Library (2004) The Wellcome Library for the History and Understanding of Medicine. London. http://library.wellcome.ac.uk/ (accessed 23 February 2004)

West, Christopher (2002) Reactions to the Research Support Libraries Group: a view from Wales, *The New Review of Academic Librarianship,* **8**: 139–151. (Note: the date of the publication is correct even though the date of publication of the report is February 2003 – see the journal editor's introduction.)

Woldering, B. (2003) *The European Library (TEL) – The Gate to Europe's Knowledge.* The European Library. http://www.europeanlibrary.org/ (accessed 2 March 2004)

WEB ADDRESSES

All addresses were accessed on 7 March 2004

Chapter 2

1. M25 Consortium http://www.m25lib.ac.uk
2. HERO http://www.hero.ac.uk/
3. London Libraries http://www.londonlibraries.org.uk/
   servlets/libraries/specialist
4. The British Library http://www.bl.uk/
5. Researcher's Gateway http://www.surrey.ac.uk/Library/
   researchers/index.shtml
6. Chetham's http://www.chethams.org.uk/
7. The London Library http://www.londonlibrary.co.uk/
8. BLPC (British Library Public Catalogue) http://blpc.bl.uk/
9. COPAC http://www.copac.ac.uk/copac/

Chapter 3

1. ZETOC http://zetoc.mimas.ac.uk/
2. SIGLE http://www.fiz-informationsdienste.de/en/DB/sigle/
   index.html

3. Royal Geographical Society http://www.rgs.org
4. British Geological Survey http://www.bgs.ac.uk/products/ digitalmaps/home.html
5. Library of Congress http://www.loc.gov/rr/microform/
6. BUBL http://www.bubl.ac.uk/
7. RDN http://www.rdn.ac.uk/

Chapter 4

1. COS http://www.cos.com/
2. CORDIS website at http://www.cordis.lu/en/home.html
3. EAGLE http://www.kb.nl/infolev/eagle/frames.htm
4. STN International http://www.stn-international.de/ stndatabases/c_datab.html
5. PhD Data http://www.PhDdata.org
6. Emerald Research Register http:// hermia.emeraldinsight.com/vl=419712/cl=38/nw=1/rpsv/ researchregister/
7. HERO http://www.hero.ac.uk/
8. Davy Faraday Research Laboratory http://www.ri.ac.uk/DFRL/
9. British Academy http://www.britac.ac.uk/arp/index.html
10. Royal Academy of Arts http://www.royalacademy.org.uk/
11. US National Academies http://www.nas.edu/
12. NATO Science Programme http://www.nato.int/science/
13. NATO RTA http://www.rta.nato.int/
14. Mannheim University http://www.uni-mannheim.de/users/ ddz/edz/net/enet.html
15. Institute of Cancer Research http://www.icr.ac.uk/
16. Action Research http://www.actionresearch.co.uk/
17. UMI Digital Dissertations http://wwwlib.umi.com/ dissertations/

Chapter 6

1. Ingenta http://www.ingenta.com/
2. APA (American Psychological Association) http:// www.apa.org/

3. National Art Library http://www.nal.vam.ac.uk/
4. National Library for the Blind http://www.nlb-online.org/
5. National Electronic Library for Health http:// www.nelh.nhs.uk/
6. National Electronic Library for Mental Health http:// www.nelmh.org/
7. BFI National Library http://www.bfi.org.uk/nationallibrary/
8. Manx National Heritage Library http://www.gov.im/mnh/ National_Library.asp
9. IALS Library http://ials.sas.ac.uk/library/library.htm
10. Institute of Electrical Engineers http://www.iee.org/TheIEE/ Research/LibSvc/index.cfm
11. RIBA (Royal Institute of British Architects) British Architectural Library http://www.architecture.com/go/ Architecture/Reference/Library_898.html
12. London Mathematical Society http://www.lms.ac.uk/
13. Natural History Museum Library http://www.nhm.ac.uk/ library/index.html
14. Royal Horticultural Society http://www.rhs.org.uk/libraries/ index.asp
15. National Oceanographic Library http://www.soc.soton.ac.uk/ LIB/
16. Centre for Ecology and Hydrology http://library.ceh.ac.uk/
17. The Courtauld Institute of Art library (also available via COPAC) http://www.courtauld.ac.uk
18. The Royal Society of Chemistry http://www.rsc.org/lic/ library.htm
19. The Royal Society http://www.royalsoc.ac.uk/
20. The Women's library http://www.thewomenslibrary.ac.uk/
21. London Business School Information Service http:// www.london.edu/library/index.html
22. WiLL http://www.londonlibraries.org.uk/will/
23. AHDS http://www.ahds.ac.uk/
24. BUFVC http://www.bufvc.ac.uk/
25. Education Image Gallery (EIG) http://edina.ac.uk/eig
26. New York Public Library http://www.nypl.org/
27. BOPCRIS http://www.bopcris.ac.uk/
28. PRO (Public Record Office) http://www.pro.gov.uk/
29. TSO http://www.tso.co.uk

Chapter 8

1. US Patent Office: Patent Full-Text and Full-Page Image Databases http://www.uspto.gov/patft/index.html
2. British Standards http://www.bsi.org.uk

Chapter 9

1. Backstage http://www.backstage.ac.uk/
2. SCONE http://scone.strath.ac.uk/service/index.cfm
3. Archives hub http://www.archiveshub.ac.uk/
4. SUNCAT project http://www.suncat.ac.uk/
5. M25 ULS http://www.m25lib.ac.uk/ULS/
6. RIDING http://riding.hostedbyfdi.net/riding/services.htm
7. SASCAT http://library.sas.ac.uk/
8. CAIRNS http://cairns.lib.strath.ac.uk
9. SALSER http://edina.ed.ac.uk/salser
10. Ebrary http://shop.ebrary.com/
11. RePEc http://repec.org/
12. AbeBooks http://www.abebooks.com/
13. Bookfinder http://www.bookfinder.com/
14. Blackwell's http://www.blackwells.co.uk
15. Amazon http://www.amazon.co.uk
16. European Information Network in the UK http://www.europe.org.uk
17. UK National Register of Archives (NRA) http://www.nra.nationalarchives.gov.uk/nra
18. AIM25 http://www.aim25.ac.uk/
19. RSLP projects http://www.rslp.ac.uk/projects/

Chapter 10

1. Northern Light http://www.northernlight.com/
2. Alta Vista http://uk.altavista.com/
3. All the Web http://www.alltheweb.com/
4. Ask Jeeves http://www.ask.com/
5. Answer Bus http://www.answerbus.com/index.shtml

6. Yahoo UK http://uk.yahoo.com
7. Ixquick http://www.ixquick.com/
8. Kartoo http://www.kartoo.com/
9. Lycos Français http://www.lycos.fr/
10. WWW.Fi http://www.fi/
11. Google UK http://www.google.co.uk
12. Teoma http://www.teoma.com
13. Vivisimo http://vivisimo.com/html/
14. Incy Wincy http://www.incywincy.com/
15. Scirus http://www.scirus.com

Chapter 11

1. Project Gutenberg http://www.gutenberg.net/index.shtml
2. SCONUL Research Extra http://www.sconul.ac.uk/use_lib/srx/
3. British Library Document Supply http://www.bl.uk/services/document/dsc.html
4. DocDel/Instant Information Systems http://www.docdel.com/
5. Kluwer http://www.wkap.nl/journal/
6. Science Direct http://www.sciencedirect.com/
7. arXiv http://arXiv.org
8. St. Andrews e-prints http://eprints.st-andrews.ac.uk/
9. Nottingham e-prints http://eprints.nottingham.ac.uk/
10. Glasgow e-prints service http://eprints.lib.gla.ac.uk/
11. Chemistry Preprint Server http://www.chemweb.com/preprint
12. E-print network http://www.osti.gov/eprints/
13. DARE http://www.surf.nl/en/themas/index2.php?oid=7
14. OAI http://www.openarchives.org/
15. BioMed Central http://www.biomedcentral.com/
16. DOAJ http://www.doaj.org/
17. PLoS http://www.publiclibraryofscience.org/
18. PubMed http://www.ncbi.nlm.nih.gov/entrez/query.fcgi?db=PubMed
19. PubMed Central http://www.pubmedcentral.nih.gov/

20. STN Easy http://stneasy.fiz-karlsruhe.de/html/english/login1.html
21. GrayLIT http://www.osti.gov/graylit/
22. BL British Thesis Service http://www.bl.uk/services/document/brittheses.html
23. NDLTD http://www.ndltd.org/
24. UKDA http://www.data-archive.ac.uk/
25. National Geophysical Data Center http://www.ngdc.noaa.gov/
26. Education Media Online http://www.emol.ac.uk/
27. AHRB Centre for British Film and Television Studies http://www.bftv.ac.uk/

Chapter 15

1. The Patent Office http://www.patent.gov.uk/
2. UK Government IP information service http://www.intellectual-property.gov.uk/
3. Community Trade Marks (EU) http://oami.eu.int/en/default.htm
4. Researcher's Companion http://www.federalsurrey.ac.uk/researcherscompanion

Chapter 16

1. SOSIG http://www.sosig.ac.uk/
2. SCENTA http://www.scenta.co.uk/
3. Times Higher Education Supplement http://www.thes.co.uk/
4. All Conferences http://www.allconferences.com/
5. Conference Alerts http://www.conferencealerts.com/
6. Open University Press http://mcgraw-hill.co.uk/openup/
7. Sage http://www.sagepub.co.uk/
8. OUP http://www.oup.co.uk
9. Springer Link http://www.springerlink.com
10. InfoTrieve http://www4.infotrieve.com/home.asp
11. American Association for the Advancement of Science (AAAS) http://www.eurekalert.org/

12. Jiscmail http://www.jiscmail.ac.uk/
13. LISTERV http://www.lsoft.com/
14. Researchers Forum http://www.researchersforum.gov.uk/

Chapter 17

1. JISC Join-up projects http://edina.ac.uk/projects/joinup/about.shtml
2. Company of Biologists http://www.biologists.com/web/
3. eBank UK http://www.ukoln.ac.uk/projects/ebank-uk/
4. SPARC Europe http://www.sparceurope.org/
5. Theses Alive! http://www.thesesalive.ac.uk/
6. ETD http://www.lib.gla.ac.uk/daedalus/
7. Digital Curation Centre http://www.jisc.ac.uk/index.cfm?name=dcc_news_040204

INDEX